101 Swimming Lesson Plans

for swimming teachers

Ready-made lesson plans for swimming teachers that take the hard work out of planning

Mark Young

A Catalogue record for this book is available from the British Library

ISBN 9780995484269

Published by: Educate & Learn Publishing, Hertfordshire, UK

Design and typeset by Mark Young

Published in association with www.swim-teach.com

Note: This book is intended for guidance and support only. The material contained here should accompany additional course material set on an official swimming teaching course by an official Swimming Association. Neither the author nor the publisher can accept responsibility for any injury or loss sustained as a result of the use of this material.

Author Online!
For more resources and swimming help visit
Mark Young's website at

www.swim-teach.com

Mark Young is a well-established swimming instructor with decades of experience teaching thousands of adults and children to swim. He has taken nervous, frightened children and adults that fear water and made them happy and confident swimmers. He has also turned many of average ability into advanced swimmers. This book draws on his experiences and countless successes to bring together lesson plans that are simple to follow, easy to adapt and ensure progress.

Also by Mark Young

Teaching Guides
How To Be A Swimming Teacher
How To Teach Front Crawl
How To Teach Breaststroke
How To Teach Backstroke
How To Teach Butterfly

Learn to Swim Guides
The Complete Beginners Guide to Swimming
How To Swim Front Crawl
How To Swim Breaststroke
How To Swim Backstroke
How To Swim Butterfly
The Swimming Strokes Book

Contents

'By failing to prepare you are preparing to fail.'

This famous quote by Benjamin Franklin is valid in all walks of life, but none more than when it comes to teaching. Careful and detailed planning is essential for delivering practical, results-based swimming lessons.

We all know that students that come to the pool for lessons come in all shapes and sizes. As swimming teachers, we encounter pupils of different ages and personalities. They all come with a level of built-in confidence or fear - depending on their history.

The lesson plans in this book are simply *guidelines* and they can therefore be adapted and changed according to the student or group of students you have in your lessons.

<u>NOTE:</u> These lesson plans are designed to be delivered by a qualified swimming instructor as part of an organised swimming school or association.

An electronic version of this book is available at:

www.swim-teach.com

How To Use This Book

Lesson Plan Layout

Lesson Plan #2

Lesson type: full stroke front crawl
Level: adult or child intermediate
Previous learning: basic front crawl technique
Lesson aim: to progress and develop the whole stroke
Equipment: floats, pull buoys, sinkers and hoop

Lesson type: the part of front crawl that this lesson focuses on. For example, **Front Crawl Breathing Technique**.

Level: who the lesson is aimed at if they are beginners, intermediate or advanced level. For example, **Child Beginner.**

Previous learning: the aspects of swimming the pupil is expected to have covered before this lesson. For example, **basic front paddle**. The pupil is *not* expected to have completely mastered an aspect of swimming but should have had some experience of learning it.

Lesson aim: the lesson objective or desired outcome of the lesson. For example, **'to learn basic breaststroke leg kick'**.

Equipment: the equipment you will need for this lesson. For example, **'floats, buoyancy aids and hoop'**. The use of buoyancy aids for any lesson is at the discretion of the teacher. Some pupils may need more than others.

Lesson Sequences

Lesson plans are laid out in a sequence (beginner, intermediate, advanced) to give the teacher easy reference to other lessons, exercises and activities in that sequence. This should allow for easier differentiation across varying abilities. Lesson plans do not have to be followed in sequence, although they can be if you wish. Each plan has its own aim and therefore can be used in sequence with other lessons aimed at that level, to suit the individual pupil or pupils.

These lesson plans and the exercises and activities in them are set out as a guide. Every pupil is different and will interpret and respond to exercises and teaching points in their own way, therefore as a swimming teacher it is important to be flexible in your approach. In other words, where a pupil is finding a particular exercise difficult, chose an easier exercise from a previous plan. Where a pupil is not quite grasping the concept of what you are teaching, try using a different phrase or teaching point.

Teaching Points

Teaching points are our 'magic words'. Having a variety of them in our virtual tool kit can be extremely useful. For example, when you say to a pupil 'point your toes and they just don't get it, you change the teaching point to 'kick with floppy feet'. All of sudden they are kicking with relaxed ankles and pointed toes.

Learning to be creative with our teaching points can be a very powerful skill and can be the difference between a pupil struggling and that light bulb moment when they suddenly understand and can do it.

Organising Your Swimmers

The way you chose to organise your swimmers as they swim off to perform a given exercise is vital to maintaining a safe learning environment and to monitor their progress.

The organisation column of the lesson plans make a suggestion but you will have to use your professional judgement, based on the size of your class and swimming lesson area available in your pool.

The suggestions are:

All together - you instruct all swimmers to go at the same time. Ideal if you have sufficient space and can be unsafe if you do not.

Waves - number your swimmers 1 and 2 alternately (or more if you have a large class). Then instruct all numbers 1's to go first, followed by the number 2's and so on if you have more. This is a good way of monitoring swimmers and also a great way to organise large classes of advanced swimmers.

One-by-one - sending each swimmer off one at a time. This is an ideal way to closely monitor each pupil.

Getting The Timing Right

All swimming pools vary in their dimensions and often larger pools have an area roped off for swimming lessons, so the whole pool is rarely used. These plans assume that beginner and intermediate swimmers will swim widths and advanced swimmers will swim lengths. The size of the width and length in *your* pool might not fit with how these plans are formatted and you may wish to use your professional judgment to change them to fit with your circumstances.

The duration of most swimming lessons is about 30 minutes. The timings of each exercise in these lesson plans are a guide and again, your professional judgement can be used to adjust them to suit your pupils and your pool size.

If you begin to discover that you are racing through the lesson and will have time left over, remember any exercise can be repeated. Repeating an exercise will enhance a pupil's strength, stamina and overall ability. A different teaching point can also be used to help those that perhaps did not quite get it the first time around.

Useful Terminology:

Beginner - a pupil just starting to learn a skill who has little or no previous experience. This could also be a pupil who has some experience but has not yet reached an intermediate standard.

Intermediate - a pupil who has progressed beyond beginner level but has not yet reached an advanced level.

Advanced - a pupil who has progressed beyond an intermediate level.

Shallow water - a water level that is at or below the height of the pupil's chest.

Deep water - a water level that is such that the pupil cannot stand on the pool floor without becoming submerged.

Prone - 'facing downwards'. For example, a prone push and glide is performed in the face-down position.

Supine - 'facing downwards' For example, a supine star float is performed on the back, facing upwards.

Bi-lateral - 'both sides'. When referring to front crawl breathing technique, the swimmer is able to roll their head to both sides to take a breath.

Lesson Plan #1

Lesson type: entering and getting used to the water
Level: child beginner
Previous learning: none
Lesson aim: to enter the water and begin to get accustomed to it
Equipment: buoyancy aids and floating toys

Exercise/Activity	Teaching Points	Organisation	Duration
Warm up: sitting on the poolside with legs in the water	move your feet slowly	all together	3 min
Main Theme: swivel entry	hands to one side and slide in on your tummy	one by one	3 mins
entry using the pool steps for those unable to perform a swivel entry	take your time	one by one	3 mins
walking through shallow water	small steps	all together	2 mins
walking backwards through the water	slide your feet	all together	3 mins
walking to collect a toy and return it	take you time	waves	3 mins
holding the poolside, bouncing up and down	slowly at first	all together	3 mins
jumping through the water to collect a toy	small jumps	waves	3 mins
Contrasting Activity: splashing and throwing water into the air	splash with your hands	all together	2 mins
blowing bubbles at the water surface	blow gently	all together	2 mins
Exit: using the pool steps	take your time	one by one	1 min

Total time: 28 minutes

Lesson #1 Assessment

Lesson Objective: to enter the water and begin to get accustomed to it		
Below average	**Average**	**Above average**
🙂	🙂	😎
Attempts to demonstrate but does not show the correct technique	Able to perform most of the technique correctly some of the time	Performs the technique correctly most of the time

Assessment	🙂	🙂	😎
Enters the water			
Walk through shallow water			
Walk backwards through shallow water			
Jump through the water			
Splash the water			

Lesson Plan #2

Lesson type: getting used to the water
Level: child beginner
Previous learning: entering the water using the pool steps
Lesson aim: to get used to wetting the face and moving around in the water
Equipment: buoyancy aids, floating toys and watering cans

Exercise/Activity	Teaching Points	Organisation	Duration
Entry: swivel entry or using the pool steps	take your time	all together	1 min
Warm up: holding the poolside, bouncing up and down	slowly at first	all together	2 mins
walking to collect a toy and return it	take your time	one by one	3 mins
jumping through the water to collect a toy	small jumps	all together	2 mins
splashing water into the air	catch the water	all together	3 mins
pretending to wash the face	wet your hands and wet your face	all together	2 mins
blowing a toy across the water surface	deep breath and blow	all together	3 mins
blowing bubbles at the water surface	blow gently	waves	3 mins
Contrasting Activity: washing hair with a watering can	close your eyes	one by one	3 mins
holding the poolside and kicking the legs	splash your feet	waves	3 mins
Exit: using the pool steps	take your time	one by one	1 min

Total time: 26 minutes

Lesson #2 Assessment

Lesson Objective: to get used to wetting the face and moving around in the water		
Below average	**Average**	**Above average**
😐	🙂	😎
Attempts to demonstrate but does not show the correct technique	Able to perform most of the technique correctly some of the time	Performs the technique correctly most of the time

Assessment	😐	🙂	😎
Walk through shallow water			
Jump through the water			
Wet the face			
Blow across the water surface			

Lesson Plan #3

Lesson type: confidence building
Level: child beginner
Previous learning: entering and moving around in the water
Lesson aim: to build and develop water confidence
Equipment: buoyancy aids, floating toys, sinkers, and watering cans

Exercise/Activity	Teaching Points	Organisation	Duration
Entry: swivel entry or using the pool steps	take your time	all together	1 min
Warm up: holding the poolside, bouncing up and down	slowly at first	all together	2 mins
walking through the water splashing the hands	big splashes	all together	3 mins
holding the poolside and blowing bubbles	let the bubbles tickle your nose	all together	2 mins
cupping water in hands pretending to wash the face	wash your face	all together	3 mins
sprinkling water over the head	wet your hands and wet your face	one by one	2 mins
holding the poolside and kicking the legs	splash your feet	waves	3 mins
blowing a toy across the water surface	deep breath and blow	waves	3 mins
Contrasting Activity: breath holding and submerging the mouth and nose	deep breath and hold it all in	waves	3 mins
submerging to collect an object	eyes open	one by one	3 mins
Exit: using the pool steps	take your time	one by one	1 min

Total time: 26 minutes

Lesson #3 Assessment

Lesson Objective: to build and develop water confidence		
Below average	**Average**	**Above average**
😐	🙂	😎
Attempts to demonstrate but does not show the correct technique	**Able to perform most of the technique correctly some of the time**	**Performs the technique correctly most of the time**

Assessment	😐	🙂	😎
Walk through shallow water			
Wets their hands and then face			
Allows water to be sprinkled over the head			
Blows bubbles at the water surface			
Kicks legs and makes a splash			

Lesson Plan #4

Lesson type: confidence building
Level: child beginner
Previous learning: moving around in the water and blowing bubbles
Lesson aim: develop water confidence by introducing breathing and submerging
Equipment: buoyancy aids, floating toys and sinkers

Exercise/Activity	Teaching Points	Organisation	Duration
Entry: swivel entry or using the pool steps	take your time	all together	1 min
Warm up: holding the poolside and kicking the legs	splash your feet	all together	2 mins
holding the poolside and blowing bubbles	blow gently	all together	2 mins
cupping water in hands pretending to wash the face	wash your face	waves	2 mins
breath holding and submerging the mouth and nose	deep breath and hold it all in	all together	3 mins
kicking legs and blowing bubbles (holding the poolside, assisted or with buoyancy aids)	kick and blow	waves	4 mins
kicking with buoyancy aids to collect a toy (with assistance)	floppy feet	waves	4 mins
kicking and blowing a toy along the surface	kick and blow gently	waves	3 mins
Contrasting Activity: assisted sitting dive, face up (with buoyancy aids and/or support from teacher or assistant)	lay your chin on the water	one by one	3 mins
submerging to collect an object	eyes open	one by one	3 mins
Exit: using the pool steps	take your time	one by one	1 min

Total time: 28 minutes

Lesson #4 Assessment

Lesson Objective: develop water confidence by introducing breathing and submerging		
Below average	**Average**	**Above average**
😐	🙂	😎
Attempts to demonstrate but does not show the correct technique	**Able to perform most of the technique correctly some of the time**	**Performs the technique correctly most of the time**

Assessment	😐	🙂	😎
Blows bubbles at the water surface			
Wets their hands and then face			
Submerges the mouth			
Submerges the mouth and nose			
Kicks legs and blows bubbles			

Lesson Plan #5

Lesson type: confidence building

Level: child beginner
Previous learning: partial submersion and blowing bubbles
Lesson aim: develop water confidence using independence and regaining standing
Equipment: buoyancy aids, floating toys and sinkers

Exercise/Activity	Teaching Points	Organisation	Duration
Entry: swivel entry or using the pool steps	take your time	all together	1 min
Warm up: holding the poolside and kicking the legs	splash your feet	all together	2 mins
breath holding and submerging the mouth and nose	hold your breath	all together	2 mins
kicking legs and blowing bubbles (holding the poolside, assisted or with buoyancy aids)	kick and blow	waves	2 mins
kicking with buoyancy aids to collect a toy (with assistance if needed)	floppy feet	waves	4 mins
kicking with buoyancy aids and independently regain standing at various points	knees to chest and stand	waves	4 mins
submerge face to collect a toy or object	eyes open	waves	4 mins
kicking with buoyancy aids, submerge the face and regain standing	deep breath and kick	waves	3 mins
Contrasting Activity: floating on the back with buoyancy aids	look up and relax	waves	3 mins
jump in from standing (with buoyancy aids if needed)	jump away from the side	one by one	3 mins
Exit: using the pool steps	take your time	one by one	1 min

Total time: 29 minutes

Lesson #5 Assessment

Lesson Objective: develop water confidence using independence and regaining standing		
Below average	**Average**	**Above average**
😐	🙂	😎
Attempts to demonstrate but does not show the correct technique	**Able to perform most of the technique correctly some of the time**	**Performs the technique correctly most of the time**

Assessment	😐	🙂	😎
Holds their breath			
Holds their breath and submerges			
Attempts to stand whilst kicking			
Submerges to collect an object			
Submerges the face whilst kicking			

Lesson Plan #6

Lesson type: floating and gliding
Level: child beginner
Previous learning: face submersion and regaining standing
Lesson aim: to learn and gain confidence in floating and gliding
Equipment: buoyancy aids and sinkers

Exercise/Activity	Teaching Points	Organisation	Duration
Entry: swivel entry or using the pool steps	take your time	all together	1 min
Warm up: 2 widths with buoyancy aids (assisted if necessary)	splash your feet	all together	2 mins
Main theme: push and glide towards the side and regain standing with buoyancy aids as needed	legs together	one by one	3 mins
push and glide away from the the side and regain standing with buoyancy aids as needed	stretch arms in front	one by one	3 mins
supine star float with buoyancy aids as needed	tummy up	waves	3 mins
prone star float with buoyancy aids as needed	face in the water	waves	4 mins
push and glide on the back, away from the side	look up at the sky	waves	3 mins
mushroom float and regain standing	chin on chest	waves	3 mins
Contrasting Activity: pencil jump (with buoyancy aids if needed)	arms by sides	waves	3 mins
submerge to collect a toy or object	deep breath and stretch down	one by one	3 mins
Exit: using the pool steps	take your time	one by one	1 min

Total time: 29 minutes

Lesson #6 Assessment

Lesson Objective: to learn and gain confidence in floating and gliding		
Below average	**Average**	**Above average**
😐	🙂	😎
Attempts to demonstrate but does not show the correct technique	**Able to perform most of the technique correctly some of the time**	**Performs the technique correctly most of the time**

Assessment	😐	🙂	😎
Regain standing with buoyancy aids			
Confidently push away from the poolside			
Float in a supine position (with aids if needed)			
Float in a prone position (with aids if needed)			
Regain standing from a floating position			

Lesson Plan #7

Lesson type: front paddle
Level: child beginner
Previous learning: kicking legs and some floating
Lesson aim: to learn the basic movements needed for front paddle
Equipment: buoyancy aids and sinkers

Exercise/Activity	Teaching Points	Organisation	Duration
Entry: swivel entry or using the pool steps	take your time	all together	1 min
Warm up: 2 widths with buoyancy aids (assisted if necessary)	splash your feet	all together	2 mins
Main theme: push and glide using a woggle	push off like a rocket	one by one	3 mins
sitting on the poolside edge kicking	pointed toes	all together	2 mins
kicking using a float under each arm	floppy feet	waves	3 mins
standing on the poolside practicing arms	reach and pull	all together	2 mins
walking through the water with arm actions	fingers together	waves	3 mins
walking through the water, using arms and blowing bubbles	blow gently as you pull	waves	3 mins
Contrasting Activity: supine star float	relax and stretch out	waves	3 mins
submerge to collect a toy or object	deep breath and stretch down	one by one	3 mins
Exit: using the pool steps	take your time	one by one	1 min

Total time: 26 minutes

Lesson #7 Assessment

Lesson Objective: to learn the basic movements needed for front paddle		
Below average	**Average**	**Above average**
😐	🙂	😎
Attempts to demonstrate but does not show the correct technique	Able to perform most of the technique correctly some of the time	Performs the technique correctly most of the time

Assessment	😐	🙂	😎
Leg kick is alternating			
Kicks with relaxed ankles			
Leg kick provides some propulsion			
Uses arms in a pulling action			

Lesson Plan #8

Lesson type: front paddle
Level: child beginner
Previous learning: basic front kicking and pulling action
Lesson aim: to learn and develop an independent front paddle
Equipment: buoyancy aids, floaters and sinkers

Exercise/Activity	Teaching Points	Organisation	Duration
Entry: swivel entry or using the pool steps	take your time	all together	1 min
Warm up: 2 widths with buoyancy aids	kick and pull	all together	2 mins
Main theme: push and glide using 2 floats	chin on the water	one by one	3 mins
holding the poolside and kicking	straight legs	all together	2 mins
kicking using a float under each arm, chasing a floating toy	kick fast	waves	3 mins
kicking and pulling using a woggle, chase a toy if needed	reach and pull	waves	3 mins
push and glide using a woggle, adding arm pulls	stretch out and pull	waves	3 mins
push off from pool floor, kick and pull towards the poolside (distance from side can vary).	chin down, toes up	waves	4 mins
Contrasting Activity: standing jump from the poolside (assisted if needed)	jump away from the side	one by one	3 mins
submerge to collect a toy or object	deep breath and stretch down	one by one	3 mins
Exit: using the pool steps	take your time	one by one	1 min

Total time: 28 minutes

Lesson #8 Assessment

Lesson Objective: to learn and develop an independent front paddle		
Below average	**Average**	**Above average**
😐	🙂	😎
Attempts to demonstrate but does not show the correct technique	**Able to perform most of the technique correctly some of the time**	**Performs the technique correctly most of the time**

Assessment	😐	🙂	😎
Leg kick is alternating and continuous			
Kicks with relaxed ankles			
Leg kick provides some propulsion			
Arm action is alternating			
Arm action provides propulsion			

Lesson Plan #9

Lesson type: front paddle
Level: child beginner
Previous learning: basic front kicking and pulling action
Lesson aim: to develop an independent front paddle
Equipment: buoyancy aids and sinkers

Exercise/Activity	Teaching Points	Organisation	Duration
Entry: swivel entry or using the pool steps	take your time	all together	1 min
Warm up: 2 widths with buoyancy aids	kick and pull	all together	2 mins
Main theme: push and glide with no floats	face in the water	one by one	3 mins
kicking holding a float	pointed toes	waves	3 mins
kicking with a float under one arm, adding arm pulls	fingers together	waves	3 mins
kicking and pulling using a woggle with face in the water	scoop for ice-cream	waves	3 mins
push and glide, adding arm pulls and leg kicks	chin down, toes up	waves	3 mins
push and glide, adding arm pulls and leg kicks, with face in the water	deep breath and kick fast	waves	3 mins
Contrasting Activity: standing jump from the poolside and swim through a floating hoop	jump away from the side	one by one	3 mins
supine star float	stretch out, chest up	waves	3 mins
Exit: using the pool steps	take your time	one by one	1 min

Total time: 28 minutes

Lesson #9 Assessment

Lesson Objective: to develop an independent front paddle		
Below average	**Average**	**Above average**
😐	🙂	😎
Attempts to demonstrate but does not show the correct technique	**Able to perform most of the technique correctly some of the time**	**Performs the technique correctly most of the time**

Assessment	😐	🙂	😎
Leg kick is alternating and continuous			
Kicks with relaxed ankles with toes pointed			
Chin remains on the water surface			
Arm action is alternating and continuous			
Able to swim a predetermined distance*			

*distance should be set on a pupil by pupil basis and the teacher should use their professional judgement to set this as means of encouragement.

Lesson Plan #10

Lesson type: back paddle
Level: child beginner
Previous learning: basic alternating kicking and supine floating
Lesson aim: to learn a basic back paddle
Equipment: buoyancy aids and hoop

Exercise/Activity	Teaching Points	Organisation	Duration
Entry: swivel entry or using the pool steps	take your time	all together	1 min
Warm up: 2 widths with buoyancy aids	kick and pull	all together	2 mins
Main theme: push and glide with a woggle	look up to the sky	waves	3 mins
sitting on the poolside kicking	pointed toes	all together	3 mins
supine kicking with a woggle	floppy feet	waves	3 mins
sitting on the poolside practicing the arm action	stroke the dog	waves	3 mins
supine kicking with a woggle, adding arm pulls	fingers together	waves	3 mins
push and glide, adding arm pulls and leg kicks and breathing	relax and breathe	waves	3 mins
Contrasting Activity: mushroom float for a set time (10 s for example)	chin on your chest	waves	3 mins
prone push and glide through a hoop	stretch out and glide	one by one	3 mins
Exit: using the pool steps	take your time	one by one	1 min

Total time: 28 minutes

Lesson #10 Assessment

Lesson Objective: to learn a basic back paddle		
Below average	**Average**	**Above average**
😐	🙂	😎
Attempts to demonstrate but does not show the correct technique	**Able to perform most of the technique correctly some of the time**	**Performs the technique correctly most of the time**

Assessment	😐	🙂	😎
Leg kick is alternating			
Kicks are relaxed			
Head is back, eyes facing upwards			
Arm action is relaxed			

Lesson Plan #11

Lesson type: back paddle
Level: child beginner
Previous learning: basic kicking and arm action on the back with aids
Lesson aim: to develop an independent back paddle
Equipment: buoyancy aids and sinkers

Exercise/Activity	Teaching Points	Organisation	Duration
Entry: swivel entry or using the pool steps	take your time	all together	1 min
Warm up: 2 widths with buoyancy aids	kick and pull	all together	2 mins
Main theme: supine push and glide	push your chest up	one by one	3 mins
kicking using a float under each arm	kick from your hips	waves	3 mins
kicking with a float held on the chest	flick your toes up	waves	3 mins
supine kicking with a woggle adding arm pulls	polish the water	waves	3 mins
supine push and glide, adding arm pulls and leg kicks	head back, chest up	waves	3 mins
push and glide into back paddle, increasing the distance of the swim	continuous arms and legs	waves	3 mins
Contrasting Activity: submerge to collect an object	eyes open	one by one	3 mins
jump in and swim through a hoop	jump away from the poolside	one by one	3 mins
Exit: using the pool steps	take your time	one by one	1 min

Total time: 28 minutes

Lesson #11 Assessment

Lesson Objective: to develop an independent back paddle		
Below average	**Average**	**Above average**
😐	🙂	😎
Attempts to demonstrate but does not show the correct technique	Able to perform most of the technique correctly some of the time	Performs the technique correctly most of the time

Assessment	😐	🙂	😎
Leg kick is alternating and continuous			
Kicks with relaxed ankles and pointed toes			
Head is back			
Chest and hips are up			
Arm action is relaxed with fingers together			
Able to swim a predetermined distance*			

*distance should be set on a pupil by pupil basis and the teacher should use their professional judgement to set this as means of encouragement.

Lesson Plan #12

Lesson type: dolphin kick
Level: child beginner
Previous learning: basic kicking and face submersion
Lesson aim: to begin learning a basic dolphin kicking action
Equipment: buoyancy aids, floats, hoop, sinkers

Exercise/Activity	Teaching Points	Organisation	Duration
Entry: swivel entry or using the pool steps	take your time	all together	1 min
Warm up: 2 widths with buoyancy aids if needed	kick and pull	all together	2 mins
Main theme: standing on the poolside practicing an undulating hip action	move your hips back and forth	all together	2 mins
sitting on a woggle, swing legs backwards and forwards	kick both legs at the same time	waves	3 mins
float under each arm kicking in a vertical position	kick hard and rise up	waves	3 mins
supine push and glide adding kicks	flick your feet up	waves	3 mins
prone push and glide adding kicks	wriggle like a worm	waves	3 mins
dolphin kick over an increased distance, adding breathing	kick like a mermaid	waves	3 mins
Contrasting Activity: collect small floating object and return it to the poolside	chin down and toes up	waves	3 mins
swim through a submerged hoop and collect an object	jump away from the poolside	one by one	3 mins
Exit: using the pool steps	take your time	one by one	1 min

Total time: 27 minutes

Lesson #12 Assessment

Lesson Objective: to begin learning a basic dolphin kicking action		
Below average	**Average**	**Above average**
😐	🙂	😎
Attempts to demonstrate but does not show the correct technique	**Able to perform most of the technique correctly some of the time**	**Performs the technique correctly most of the time**

Assessment	😐	🙂	😎
Performs an undulating hip action			
Legs kick simultaneously			
Whole body movement is 'wave-like'			
Movement is relaxed and flowing			

Lesson Plan #13

Lesson type: shallow water skills
Level: child beginner
Previous learning: floating, submerging and regaining the feet
Lesson aim: enhance water confidence by linking shallow water skills
Equipment: buoyancy aids if needed

Exercise/Activity	Teaching Points	Organisation	Duration
Entry: swivel entry or using the pool steps	take your time	all together	1 min
Warm up: swim 2 widths any stroke	kick with floppy feet	all together	2 mins
Main theme: prone push and glide and regain standing	relax and stand	waves	3 mins
supine push and glide, regaining standing	hips and chest up	waves	3 mins
prone push and glide, rotating onto the back	floppy feet	waves	3 mins
supine push and glide and return to the start using front paddle	face down on the way back	waves	3 mins
prone push and glide and return to the start, kicking in a supine position	head back, hips up on the way back	waves	3 mins
swim away from the poolside, change direction and return to the start	face down and kick continuously	waves	3 mins
Contrasting Activity: introduce head first sculling	fingers together, wrists firm	waves	3 mins
introduce treading water in water of shoulder depth	eyes and ears out of the water	one by one	3 mins
Exit: using the pool steps	take your time	one by one	1 min

Total time: 28 minutes

Lesson #13 Assessment

Lesson Objective: enhance water confidence by linking shallow water skills

Below average	Average	Above average
😐	🙂	😎
Attempts to demonstrate but does not show the correct technique	Able to perform most of the technique correctly some of the time	Performs the technique correctly most of the time

Assessment	😐	🙂	😎
Push and glide from a prone position			
Push and glide from a supine position			
Regain standing position from prone position			
Regain standing position from supine position			
Rotate from supine to prone position whilst swimming			
Return to the poolside from a push and glide			

Lesson Plan #14

Lesson type: swimming in deep water
Level: child beginner
Previous learning: basic front paddle, submerging and floating
Lesson aim: to gain confidence in swimming out of depth
Equipment: buoyancy aids if needed

Exercise/Activity	Teaching Points	Organisation	Duration
Entry: swivel entry or using the pool steps	take your time	all together	1 min
Warm up: swim 2 widths any stroke (within depth)	kick with floppy feet	all together	2 mins
Main theme: prone push and glide and return to the start without touching the pool floor	toes up and kick	waves	3 mins
supine push and glide and return to the start without touching the pool floor	face down on the way back	waves	3 mins
swim away from poolside, change direction and return without touching pool floor	face down and kick continuously	waves	3 mins
DEEP WATER: jump away from the poolside and return swimming front paddle	jump away from the side	waves	3 mins
DEEP WATER: swim a predetermined distance from deep to shallow water	relax and take your time	waves	3 mins
DEEP WATER: swim front paddle showing 2 changes of direction	continuous kicking and pulling	waves	3 mins
Contrasting Activity: feet first surface dive	stretch up tall and then sink	waves	3 mins
head first surface dive	head down, hips up	waves	3 mins
Exit: using the pool steps	take your time	one by one	1 min

Total time: 28 minutes

Lesson #14 Assessment

Lesson Objective: to gain confidence in swimming out of depth		
Below average	**Average**	**Above average**
😐	🙂	😎
Attempts to demonstrate but does not show the correct technique	Able to perform most of the technique correctly some of the time	Performs the technique correctly most of the time

Assessment	😐	🙂	😎
Return to the poolside from a push and glide			
Return to the poolside from a supine position			
Jump into deep water			
Swim from deep water to shallow			

Lesson Plan #15

Lesson type: deep water skills
Level: child beginner
Previous learning: basic front paddle, submerging and floating
Lesson aim: to enhance confidence when swimming in deep water
Equipment: woggles and sinkers if needed

Exercise/Activity	Teaching Points	Organisation	Duration
Entry: swivel entry or using the pool steps	take your time	all together	1 min
Warm up: swim 2 widths any stroke (within depth)	kick with floppy feet	all together	2 mins
Main theme: DEEP WATER: jump away from the poolside and return swimming front paddle	jump away from the side	waves	3 mins
swim a predetermined distance from deep to shallow water	continuous kicking and pulling	waves	3 mins
kicking vertically (treading water) using a woggle between the legs	keep your head above the surface	waves	3 mins
treading water for a set time (30, 45 or 60 seconds)	keep ears and eyes above the surface	waves	3 mins
treading water followed by a head first surface dive	deep breath and dig down deep	waves	3 mins
treading water followed by a surface dive and swim underwater	relax and conserve your energy	waves	3 mins
Contrasting Activity: head first sculling	push the water to your feet	all together	3 mins
feet first sculling	toes and hips up	waves	3 mins
Exit: using the pool steps	take your time	one by one	1 min

Total time: 28 minutes

Lesson #15 Assessment

Lesson Objective: to enhance confidence when swimming in deep water		
Below average	**Average**	**Above average**
😐	🙂	😎
Attempts to demonstrate but does not show the correct technique	Able to perform most of the technique correctly some of the time	Performs the technique correctly most of the time

Assessment	😐	🙂	😎
Return to the poolside from a jump			
Swim from deep water to shallow			
Tread water for a predetermined time			
Tread water and then surface dive			
Tread water, surface dive and then swim submerged			

Lesson Plan #16

Lesson type: getting used to the water

Level: adult beginner
Previous learning: none
Lesson aim: to get used to being in the water
Equipment: buoyancy aids

Exercise/Activity	Teaching Points	Organisation	Duration
Entry: using the pool steps	take your time	all together	1 min
Warm up: walking in water of waist depth (holding the poolside if needed)	slowly at first	all together	2 mins
holding the poolside, sink down to submerge the shoulders	relax and breathe	all together	2 mins
walking into deeper water (up to shoulder depth if able)	take your time	all together	3 mins
holding the poolside, blow bubbles at the surface	breathe out slowly and gently	all together	3 mins
holding the poolside, breath holding and submerging the mouth then nose (eyes if comfortable)	relax and take your time	all together	2 mins
Moving through the water at shoulder depth, blowing bubbles	raise the mouth to inhale	all together	3 mins
Moving through water at shoulder depth, changing direction, moving backwards	relax and take your time	all together	3 mins
Contrasting Activity: holding the poolside and kicking the legs	relax your knees and ankles	waves	3 mins
Choose one exercise from this lesson to repeat	choose something you found tricky	one by one	4 mins
Exit: using the pool steps	take your time	one by one	2 min

Total time: 28 minutes

Lesson #16 Assessment

Lesson Objective: to get used to being in the water		
Below average	**Average**	**Above average**
😐	🙂	😎
Attempts to demonstrate but does not show the correct technique	Able to perform most of the technique correctly some of the time	Performs the technique correctly most of the time

Assessment	😐	🙂	😎
Walk through shallow water			
Walk into deeper water			
Exhale into the water			
Move through the water, changing direction			

Lesson Plan #17

Lesson type: floating and gliding

Level: adult beginner
Previous learning: being used to the water and face submerging
Lesson aim: to learn and gain confidence in floating and gliding
Equipment: woggles, floats and other buoyancy aids if needed

Exercise/Activity	Teaching Points	Organisation	Duration
Entry: using the pool steps	take your time	all together	1 min
Warm up: Moving through the water at shoulder depth, blowing bubbles	relax and blow	all together	2 mins
Main theme: prone star float with buoyancy aids or teacher support as needed	face in the water	one by one	3 mins
push and glide towards the side and regain standing with buoyancy aids as needed	legs together	waves	3 mins
push and glide away from the the side and regain standing with buoyancy aids as needed	stretch arms in front	waves	3 mins
supine star float with buoyancy aids or teacher support as needed	head back and relax	one by one	3 mins
push and glide on the back, away from the side	chest and hips up	waves	3 mins
mushroom float and regain standing	chin on chest	waves	3 mins
Contrasting Activity: push and glide adding kicking	slow relaxed kicks	waves	3 mins
Choose one exercise from this lesson to repeat	choose something you found tricky	one by one	4 mins
Exit: using the pool steps	take your time	one by one	1 min

Total time: 29 minutes

Lesson #17 Assessment

Lesson Objective: to learn and gain confidence in floating and gliding		
Below average	**Average**	**Above average**
😐	🙂	😎
Attempts to demonstrate but does not show the correct technique	Able to perform most of the technique correctly some of the time	Performs the technique correctly most of the time

Assessment	😐	🙂	😎
Regain standing with buoyancy aids			
Glide towards the poolside			
Float in a supine position (with aids if needed)			
Float in a prone position (with aids if needed)			
Regain standing from a floating position			
Glide away from the poolside and regain standing			

Lesson Plan #18

Lesson type: front paddle
Level: adult beginner
Previous learning: kicking legs, gliding and floating
Lesson aim: to learn the basic movements needed for front paddle
Equipment: buoyancy aids as needed

Exercise/Activity	Teaching Points	Organisation	Duration
Entry: using the pool steps	take your time	all together	1 min
Warm up: Moving through the water at shoulder depth, blowing bubbles	relax and get used to the water	all together	2 mins
Main theme: push and glide using buoyancy aids if needed	push off and stretch out	waves	3 mins
holding the poolside kicking	relaxed knees and ankles	all together	2 mins
kicking using a float under each arm	floppy feet	waves	3 mins
walking through the water with arm actions	fingers together	all together	2 mins
kicking and pulling using a woggle	reach and pull	waves	3 mins
push and glide using a woggle, adding arm pulls and leg kicks	feel your way through the water	waves	3 mins
Contrasting Activity: supine star float	relax and stretch out	waves	3 mins
push and glide in a supine position, using buoyancy aids as needed	head back, chest and hips up	waves	3 mins
Exit: using the pool steps	take your time	one by one	2 min

Total time: 27 minutes

Lesson #18 Assessment

Lesson Objective: to learn the basic movements needed for front paddle		
Below average	**Average**	**Above average**
😐	🙂	😎
Attempts to demonstrate but does not show the correct technique	**Able to perform most of the technique correctly some of the time**	**Performs the technique correctly most of the time**

Assessment	😐	🙂	😎
Leg kick is alternating			
Leg kick provides some propulsion			
Uses arms in a pulling action			
Uses arms and legs simultaneously			

Lesson Plan #19

Lesson type: front paddle
Level: adult beginner
Previous learning: basic alternating front kicking and pulling action
Lesson aim: to learn and develop an independent front paddle
Equipment: woggles and buoyancy aids as needed

Exercise/Activity	Teaching Points	Organisation	Duration
Entry: swivel entry or using the pool steps	take your time	all together	1 min
Warm up: kicking and pulling using a woggle	relax, kick and pull	all together	2 mins
Main theme: kicking using a float under each arm	kick with relaxed ankles	waves	3 mins
push and glide from the poolside	relax and stretch	waves	3 mins
push and glide adding leg kicks	kick from the hips	waves	3 mins
front paddle using a woggle, adding breathing	blow gently across the water	waves	3 mins
push and glide, exhaling through the glide, regain standing	relax and blow	waves	3 mins
push and glide, adding arm pulls and leg kicks, regain standing	feel your way through the water	waves	3 mins
Contrasting Activity: supine star float and regain standing	head back, chest and hips up	waves	3 mins
leg kicks in a supine position with a woggle	deep breath and stretch down	one by one	3 mins
Exit: using the pool steps	take your time	one by one	2 min

Total time: 29 minutes

Lesson #19 Assessment

Lesson Objective: to learn and develop an independent front paddle		
Below average	**Average**	**Above average**
🙂	🙂	😎
Attempts to demonstrate but does not show the correct technique	Able to perform most of the technique correctly some of the time	Performs the technique correctly most of the time

Assessment	🙂	🙂	😎
Leg kick is alternating and continuous			
Leg kick provides some propulsion			
Arm action is alternating			
Arm action provides propulsion			
Demonstrates a breathing technique			

Lesson Plan #20

Lesson type: back paddle
Level: adult beginner
Previous learning: basic alternating kicking and supine floating
Lesson aim: to learn a basic back paddle
Equipment: buoyancy aids as needed

Exercise/Activity	Teaching Points	Organisation	Duration
Entry: using the pool steps	take your time	all together	1 min
Warm up: 2 widths moving through the water (walking or swimming with aids as needed)	relax and feel the water	all together	2 mins
Main theme: push and glide with a woggle	look up to the sky	waves	3 mins
supine kicking with a woggle	pointed toes	waves	3 mins
walking backwards through the water using arm action	stroke the dog	waves	3 mins
supine kicking with a woggle, adding arm pulls, regain standing	kick from the hips	waves	3 mins
push and glide with woggle, adding arm pulls, leg kicks and regain standing	relax and breathe	waves	3 mins
supine floating, adding leg kicks and gentle arm movements - with teacher assistance as needed	relaxed gentle movements	one by one	4 mins
Contrasting Activity: supine star float, roll onto the front and regain standing	knees to your chest when standing	waves	2 mins
prone push and glide to submerge (reach the pool floor if possible)	deep breath and stretch downwards	waves	3 mins
Exit: using the pool steps	take your time	one by one	1 min

Total time: 28 minutes

Lesson #20 Assessment

Lesson Objective: to learn a basic back paddle		
Below average	**Average**	**Above average**
😐	🙂	😎
Attempts to demonstrate but does not show the correct technique	Able to perform most of the technique correctly some of the time	Performs the technique correctly most of the time

Assessment	😐	🙂	😎
Leg kick is alternating			
Kicks are from the hips			
Head is back, eyes facing upwards			
Arm action is relaxed			

Lesson Plan #21

Lesson type: back paddle
Level: adult beginner
Previous learning: basic kicking and arm action on the back with aids
Lesson aim: to develop an independent back paddle
Equipment: buoyancy aids and sinkers

Exercise/Activity	Teaching Points	Organisation	Duration
Entry: swivel entry or using the pool steps	take your time	all together	1 min
Warm up: 2 widths with buoyancy aids if needed	relax and take your time	all together	2 mins
Main theme: supine push and glide	push your chest up	one by one	3 mins
kicking using a float under each arm	flick your toes up	waves	3 mins
supine kicking with a woggle adding arm pulls	polish the water	waves	3 mins
supine push and glide, adding arm pulls and leg kicks, regaining standing	head back, chest up	waves	3 mins
push and glide into back paddle for a short distance, regaining standing	knees to chest when standing	waves	3 mins
push and glide into back paddle, increasing distance of the swim	continuous arms and legs	waves	3 mins
Contrasting Activity: supine push and glide, roll onto the front and continue swimming prone	smooth, slow movements	waves	3 mins
submerge to collect an object	eyes open	one by one	3 mins
Exit: using the pool steps	take your time	one by one	1 min

Total time: 28 minutes

Lesson #21 Assessment

Lesson Objective: to develop an independent back paddle		
Below average	**Average**	**Above average**
😐	🙂	😎
Attempts to demonstrate but does not show the correct technique	Able to perform most of the technique correctly some of the time	Performs the technique correctly most of the time

Assessment	😐	🙂	😎
Leg kick is alternating and continuous			
Kicks with relaxed ankles and pointed toes			
Head is back			
Chest and hips are up			
Arm action is relaxed with fingers together			
Able to swim a predetermined distance*			

*distance should be set on a pupil by pupil basis and the teacher should use their professional judgement to set this as means of encouragement.

Lesson Plan #22

Lesson type: basic breaststroke
Level: adult beginner
Previous learning: front paddle and floating
Lesson aim: to learn the basics of breaststroke
Equipment: floats and woggles

Exercise/Activity	Teaching Points	Organisation	Duration
Entry: swivel or steps entry	enter slowly	all together	1 min
Warm up: 2 widths any stroke with buoyancy aids if needed	take your time	all together	3 mins
Main Theme: sitting on the poolside demonstrating kicking action	kick in a circular path	all together	2 mins
supine kicking with woggle under arms	turn out your feet	waves	3 mins
Kicking with a float under each arm	kick and glide	waves	3 mins
arm pulls, walking through shallow water	keep hands underwater	waves	4 mins
arm pulls with breathing, woggle under the arms	blow your hands forwards	waves	3 mins
full stroke, with bouyancy aids if needed	pull *then* kick	waves	3 mins
Contrasting Activity: supine star float	stretch out and relax	all together	2 mins
back paddle for a pre determined distance	relax and kick	waves	3 mins
Exit: using the pool steps or over the poolside	take your time	one by one	1 min

Total time: 28 minutes

Lesson #22 Assessment

Lesson Objective: to learn the basics of breaststroke		
Below average	**Average**	**Above average**
😐	🙂	😎
Attempts to demonstrate but does not show the correct technique	Able to perform most of the technique correctly some of the time	Performs the technique correctly most of the time

Assessment	😐	🙂	😎
Arms pull in a circular path			
Legs kick in a circular path			
Feet attempt to turn outwards			
Exhalation takes place underwater			
Arm pull and leg kick sequence is continuous			

Lesson Plan #23

Lesson type: basic breaststroke
Level: adult beginner
Previous learning: basic breaststroke technique
Lesson aim: to progress and develop basic breaststroke
Equipment: floats

Exercise/Activity	Teaching Points	Organisation	Duration
Entry: swivel or sitting dive entry	enter slowly	waves	1 min
Warm up: 2 widths any stroke	take your time	all together	3 mins
Main Theme: 2 widths full stroke breaststroke with buoyancy aids if needed	pull in a circle, kick in a circle	waves	2 mins
push and glide from the poolside	hands and feet together	one by one	3 mins
kicking with a float under each arm	knees together and kick around	waves	3 mins
kicking with a single float held in front, adding a glide after each kick	kick hard and then glide	waves	3 mins
kicking with a float, adding breathing	kick and blow out	waves	3 mins
full stroke without buoyancy aids	kick your hands into a glide	waves	3 mins
Contrasting Activity: swim and change direction without touching the pool floor	relax and take your time	waves	3 mins
Choose one exercise from this lesson to repeat	choose something you found tricky	waves	3 mins
Exit: using the pool steps or over the poolside	take your time	one by one	1 min

Total time: 28 minutes

Lesson #23 Assessment

Lesson Objective: to progress and develop basic breaststroke		
Below average	**Average**	**Above average**
😐	🙂	😎
Attempts to demonstrate but does not show the correct technique	**Able to perform most of the technique correctly some of the time**	**Performs the technique correctly most of the time**

Assessment	😐	🙂	😎
Arms pull in a small circle			
Legs kick in a circular path with knees close together			
Feet attempt to turn outwards			
A glide is attempted after each stroke			
Arms pull and legs kick in an alternating sequence.			

Lesson Plan #24

Lesson type: confidence building
Level: adult beginner
Previous learning: moving around in the water and partial submersion
Lesson aim: to increase water confidence
Equipment: buoyancy aids as needed

Exercise/Activity	Teaching Points	Organisation	Duration
Entry: swivel entry or using the pool steps	take your time	all together	1 min
Warm up: holding the poolside and kicking the legs	splash your feet	all together	2 mins
holding the poolside, exhaling at the surface - repeat*	blow gently	all together	2 mins
breath holding and submerging the mouth and nose - repeat	deep breath and hold it all in	all together	3 mins
holding the poolside, breath holding and completely submerge - repeat	slowly down and slowly up	all together	3 mins
breath holding and completely submerge without holding the poolside - repeat	relax and take your time	all together	3 mins
push and glide towards the poolside in a prone position and regain standing	stretch out and relax	waves	4 mins
prone star float and regain standing position	slow, gradual movements	waves	3 mins
Contrasting Activity: submerging to collect an object (teacher assisted by holding the object)	eyes open	one by one	3 mins
Choose one exercise from this lesson to repeat choose something you found tricky	choose something you found tricky	one by one	3 mins
Exit: using the pool steps	take your time	one by one	1 min

Total time: 28 minutes

*repetition of submersion exercises is key to enhancing confidence. Professional judgement should be used to determine the number of repetitions and the time to move on to another exercise.

Lesson #24 Assessment

Lesson Objective: to increase water confidence		
Below average	**Average**	**Above average**
😐	🙂	😎
Attempts to demonstrate but does not show the correct technique	Able to perform most of the technique correctly some of the time	Performs the technique correctly most of the time

Assessment	😐	🙂	😎
Exhale at the water surface			
Submerges the mouth and nose			
Submerges completely			
Push and glide and regain standing			
Regains standing from prone			

Lesson Plan #25

Lesson type: confidence building
Level: adult beginner
Previous learning: gliding, submersion and exhaling
Lesson aim: to develop and enhance water confidence
Equipment: buoyancy aids if needed

Exercise/Activity	Teaching Points	Organisation	Duration
Entry: using the pool steps	take your time	all together	1 min
Warm up: push and glide towards the poolside in a prone position and regain standing	slowly regain a standing position	all together	3 mins
holding the poolside, breath holding and completely submerge - repeat*	slowly down and slowly up	all together	2 mins
breath holding and completely submerge without holding the poolside - repeat	relax and take your time	waves	2 mins
push and glide from the poolside exhaling through the glide - regain standing	glide and gently blow out	waves	3 mins
prone star float and regain standing position - repeat	slow, gradual movements	waves	3 mins
supine push and glide and regain standing - repeat	knees to chest	waves	3 mins
push and glide from the poolside and return without touching the pool floor	relaxed, smooth movements	waves	3 mins
Contrasting Activity: introduce treading water (shoulder depth)	relax and keep your head up	waves	3 mins
Choose one exercise from this lesson to repeat choose something you found tricky	choose something you found tricky	one by one	3 mins
Exit: using the pool steps	take your time	one by one	1 min

Total time: 27 minutes

*repetition of certain exercises are key to enhancing confidence. Professional judgement should be used to determine the number of repetitions and the time to move on to another exercise

Lesson #25 Assessment

Lesson Objective: to develop and enhance water confidence		
Below average	**Average**	**Above average**
😐	🙂	😎
Attempts to demonstrate but does not show the correct technique	Able to perform most of the technique correctly some of the time	Performs the technique correctly most of the time

Assessment	😐	🙂	😎
Breath holds and submerges completely			
Regains a standing position from prone			
Regains a standing position from supine			
Confidently push and glide			
Returns to the poolside without touching the pool floor			

Lesson Plan #26

Lesson type: swimming in deep water
Level: adult beginner
Previous learning: basic front paddle, submerging and floating
Lesson aim: to gain confidence in swimming out of depth
Equipment: buoyancy aids if needed

Exercise/Activity	Teaching Points	Organisation	Duration
Entry: swivel entry or using the pool steps	take your time	all together	1 min
Warm up: swim 2 widths any stroke (within depth)	relaxed kicking	all together	2 mins
Main theme: prone push and glide and return to the start without touching the pool floor	toes up and kick	waves	3 mins
supine push and glide and return to the start without touching the pool floor	face down on the way back	waves	3 mins
swim away from poolside, change direction and return without touching pool floor	face down and kick continuously	waves	3 mins
DEEP WATER: push away from the poolside and return swimming front paddle	jump away from the side	waves	3 mins
DEEP WATER: swim a predetermined distance from deep to shallow water	relax and take your time	waves	3 mins
DEEP WATER: swim a predetermined distance from shallow to deep water	continuous kicking and pulling	waves	3 mins
Contrasting Activity: introduce treading water (shoulder depth)	relax and keep your head up	waves	3 mins
Choose one exercise from this lesson to repeat choose something you found tricky	choose something you found tricky	one by one	3 mins
Exit: using the pool steps	take your time	one by one	1 min

Total time: 28 minutes

Lesson #26 Assessment

Lesson Objective: to gain confidence in swimming out of depth		
Below average	**Average**	**Above average**
😐	🙂	😎
Attempts to demonstrate but does not show the correct technique	Able to perform most of the technique correctly some of the time	Performs the technique correctly most of the time

Assessment	😐	🙂	😎
Return to the poolside from a push and glide			
Return to the poolside from a supine position			
Confidently enters deep water			
Swim from deep water to shallow			
Swim from shallow water to deep			

Lesson Plan #27

Lesson type: full stroke front crawl stroke
Level: adult or child beginner
Previous learning: basic front paddle
Lesson aim: to learn each part of basic front crawl and experience the whole stroke
Equipment: floats, buoyancy aids and hoop

Exercise/Activity	Teaching Points	Organisation	Duration
Entry: swivel or steps entry	enter slowly	all together	1 min
Warm up: 2 widths any stroke with buoyancy aids if needed	take your time	all together	3 mins
Main Theme: push and glide, holding a float if needed	stretch out and glide	one by one	2 mins
kicking whilst holding a float under each arm	kick with floppy feet	all together	2 mins
single arm pull with a float held under one arm. repeat with opposite arm.	elbow leads out first	waves	4 mins
holding a float with a diagonal grip. repeat with head turning to the opposite side.	turn head to the bent elbow	waves	4 mins
alternate arm pulls holding float out in front	Count '1,2,3' each pull	waves	3 mins
full stroke front crawl	continuous arm pulls and leg kicks	waves	3 mins
Contrasting Activity: jumping entry and swim through a hoop	jump away from the side	2 or 3 at a time	3 mins
sitting dive through a hoop at the surface	head tucked down	2 or 3 at a time	3 mins
Exit: using the pool steps or over the poolside	take your time	one by one	1 min

Total time: 29 minutes

Lesson #27 Assessment

Lesson Objective: to learn each part of basic front crawl and experience the whole stroke

Below average	Average	Above average
😐	🙂	😎
Attempts to demonstrate but does not show the correct technique	Able to perform most of the technique correctly some of the time	Performs the technique correctly most of the time

Assessment	😐	🙂	😎
Face in and out of the water as they move across the pool			
Kick leg is alternating			
Arms recover over the water surface			
Able to breathe without pausing			
Leg kicks and arm pulls are continuous			

Lesson Plan #28

Lesson type: full stroke front crawl
Level: adult or child intermediate
Previous learning: basic front crawl technique
Lesson aim: to progress and develop the whole stroke to an intermediate level
Equipment: floats, pull buoys, sinkers and hoop

Exercise/Activity	Teaching Points	Organisation	Duration
Entry: swivel or sitting dive entry	enter slowly	waves	1 min
Warm up: 2 widths any stroke	take your time	all together	3 mins
Main Theme: push and glide from the side	hands and feet together	one by one	2 mins
kicking whilst holding a float in both hands	kick with long legs	waves	3 mins
arms only using a pull buoy between the legs	pull and stretch	waves	3 mins
holding a float with a diagonal grip	breathe out slowly	waves	3 mins
push and glide, add arms pulls and leg kicks	continuous arm and legs	waves	3 mins
full stroke front crawl	steady and relaxed	waves	3 mins
Contrasting Activity: head first surface dives, collecting sinkers placed apart	deep breath and dig down	one by one	3 mins
dolphin kick through a hoop at the surface	swim like a mermaid	one by one	3 mins
Exit: using the pool steps or over the poolside	take your time	one by one	1 min

Total time: 28 minutes

Lesson #28 Assessment

Lesson Objective: to progress and develop the whole stroke to an intermediate level		
Below average	**Average**	**Above average**
😐	🙂	😎
Attempts to demonstrate but does not show the correct technique	Able to perform most of the technique correctly some of the time	Performs the technique correctly most of the time

Assessment	😐	🙂	😎
Body position is horizontal			
Kick legs from the hips			
Kicks with toes pointed			
Finger and thumb enter the water first			
Head rolls to the side to breathe			
Leg kicks and arm pulls are alternating and continuous			

Lesson Plan #29

Lesson type: full stroke front crawl
Level: adult or child advanced
Previous learning: full stroke front crawl
Lesson aim: to develop and fine-tune whole stroke technique
Equipment: fins, pull buoys, hand paddles and floats

Exercise/Activity	Teaching Points	Organisation	Duration
Entry: sitting or shallow dive entry	take your time	waves	1 min
Warm up: 2 lengths front crawl	take your time	all together	3 mins
Main Theme: using fins, push and glide adding leg kicks	make your body long	waves	2 mins
kicking whilst holding a float vertically in the water	kick with floppy feet	waves	3 mins
full stroke using hand paddles	pull with power	waves	3 mins
using fins, front crawl breathing with increased time intervals	breathe out slowly	waves	3 mins
push and glide, add arms pulls and leg kicks	smooth, balanced strokes	waves	3 mins
full stroke front crawl	steady and relaxed	waves	3 mins
Contrasting Activity: dolphin kick underwater, arms by sides	lead with your head	one by one	3 mins
treading water	head above the water	waves	3 mins
Exit: using the pool steps or over the poolside	take your time	one by one	1 min

Total time: 28 minutes

Lesson #29 Assessment

Lesson Objective: to develop and fine-tune whole stroke technique		
Below average	**Average**	**Above average**
😐	🙂	😎
Attempts to demonstrate but does not show the correct technique	Able to perform most of the technique correctly some of the time	Performs the technique correctly most of the time

Assessment	😐	🙂	😎
Body position is horizontal and streamlined			
Leg kick is relaxed and rhythmical			
Kicks with toes pointed and relaxed ankles			
Arms pull to the thighs and elbow exists first			
Arm recovery is controlled and not rushed			
Breathing is regular and without pause			
Stroke timing has a continuous 6 beat cycle			

Lesson Plan #30

Lesson type: front crawl body position

Level: adult or child beginner
Previous learning: basic front paddle and submerging the face
Lesson aim: to learn basic front crawl body position
Equipment: floats, buoyancy aids and hoop

Exercise/Activity	Teaching Points	Organisation	Duration
Entry: swivel entry	enter slowly	all together	1 min
Warm up: 2 widths any stroke using buoyancy aids	take your time	all together	3 mins
Main Theme: standing, holding the poolside and submerging	deep breath and relax	all together	2 mins
holding the poolside in a horizontal position and submerging face	arms out stretched	all together	3 mins
push and glide with floats under each arm	relax and glide	one by one	4 mins
push and glide with a float held in both hands	stretch out, point toes	all together	3 mins
push and glide without buoyancy aids	hands together	waves	2 mins
push and glide adding front crawl stroke	stretch out and relax	waves	3 mins
Contrasting Activity: submerging to collect an object	take your time	2 or 3 at a time	4 mins
tuck (mushroom) float	chin and knees to chest	all together	2 mins
Exit: using the pool steps or over the poolside	take your time	one by one	1 min

Total time: 28 minutes

Lesson #30 Assessment

Lesson Objective: to learn basic front crawl body position		
Below average	**Average**	**Above average**
😐	🙂	😎
Attempts to demonstrate but does not show the correct technique	**Able to perform most of the technique correctly some of the time**	**Performs the technique correctly most of the time**

Assessment	😐	🙂	😎
Face is submerged			
Body position is flat			
Legs and feet are together			
Hands are together			
Hips are level			
Shoulders are level			

Lesson Plan #31

Lesson type: front crawl body position
Level: adult or child intermediate
Previous learning: basic front crawl technique
Lesson aim: to improve basic front crawl body position and shape
Equipment: floats and/or kickboards

Exercise/Activity	Teaching Points	Organisation	Duration
Entry: swivel entry	enter slowly	all together	1 min
Warm up: 2 widths any stroke without using buoyancy aids	take your time	all together	3 mins
Main Theme: 2 widths full stroke front crawl	relax and stretch	all together	2 mins
push and glide with a float held in both hands	feet together, toes pointed	all together	3 mins
push and glide without buoyancy aids	hands over each other	waves	3 mins
push and glide, marking distance travelled	stretch out, point toes	one by one	4 mins
push and glide, adding leg kick	hands together, stretch	waves	3 mins
push and glide adding front crawl stroke	relax and stretch	waves	3 mins
Contrasting Activity: forward somersault from a push and glide	tuck chin on chest	2 or 3 at a time	3 mins
sitting dive through a submerged hoop	hands together	2 or 3 at a time	3 mins
Exit: using the pool steps or over the poolside	take your time	one by one	1 min

Total time: 29 minutes

Lesson #31 Assessment

Lesson Objective: to improve basic front crawl body position and shape		
Below average	**Average**	**Above average**
😐	🙂	😎
Attempts to demonstrate but does not show the correct technique	**Able to perform most of the technique correctly some of the time**	**Performs the technique correctly most of the time**

Assessment	😐	🙂	😎
Face is submerged whilst moving			
Body position is horizontal			
Feet are together with toes pointed whilst moving			
Hands are together with fingers together			
Hips are level whilst moving			
Shoulders are level whilst moving			

Lesson Plan #32

Lesson type: front crawl body position

Level: adult or child advanced
Previous learning: full stroke front crawl
Lesson aim: to develop and fine-tune front crawl body position and shape
Equipment: fins

Exercise/Activity	Teaching Points	Organisation	Duration
Entry: sitting or shallow dive entry	take your time	all together	1 min
Warm up: 2 lengths any stroke	steady pace	all together	3 mins
Main Theme: 1 length full stroke front crawl	relax and stretch	all together	2 mins
push and glide from the poolside	feet together, toes pointed	all together	3 mins
push and glide, adding leg kick	hands together, stretch out	waves	3 mins
Kicking on side using fins, one arm stretched out	keep head in a neutral position	one by one	3 mins
repeat above drill on opposite side	steady kick and stretch out	waves	3 mins
push and glide adding front crawl stroke	stretch and relax	waves	3 mins
Contrasting Activity: supine push and glide and rotate to prone position	keep head level	2 or 3 at a time	3 mins
front crawl and somersault mid swim	head down, chin to chest	2 or 3 at a time	3 mins
Exit: using the pool steps or over the poolside	take your time	all together	1 min

Total time: 28 minutes

Lesson #32 Assessment

Lesson Objective: to develop and fine-tune front crawl body position and shape	

Below average	Average	Above average
😐	🙂	😎
Attempts to demonstrate but does not show the correct technique	**Able to perform most of the technique correctly some of the time**	**Performs the technique correctly most of the time**

Assessment	😐	🙂	😎
Face is submerged and head is level			
Body position is streamlined			
Body position remains streamlined whilst kicking			
Arms are stretched out and streamlined			
Hips and shoulders are level whilst moving			
Head remains in a neutral position whilst moving			

Lesson Plan #33

Lesson type: front crawl leg kick
Level: adult or child beginner
Previous learning: basic front paddle
Lesson aim: to learn basic front crawl leg kick and introduce breathing
Equipment: floats or kick-boards and buoyancy aids as necessary

Exercise/Activity	Teaching Points	Organisation	Duration
Entry: swivel entry	enter slowly	all together	1 min
Warm up: 2 widths any stroke using buoyancy aids	take your time	all together	3 mins
Main Theme: sitting the poolside demonstrating kicking action	pointed toes	all together	2 mins
holding the poolside and kicking	kick with straight legs	all together	3 mins
kicking with a float held under each arm	kick from the hips	one by one	4 mins
kicking with one float held in front	kick with floppy feet	teacher assisted	3 mins
holding the poolside blowing bubbles	blow gently	all together	2 mins
kicking with a float held under each arm adding blowing bubbles	kick and blow at the same time	all together	3 mins
Contrasting Activity: prone star float with or without a buoyancy aid	hold your breath	2 or 3 at a time	2 mins
supine star float with or without a buoyancy aid	relax and stay still	2 or 3 at a time	2 mins
Exit: using the pool steps	take your time	one by one	1 min

Total time: 26 minutes

Lesson #33 Assessment

Lesson Objective: to learn basic front crawl leg kick and introduce breathing		
Below average	**Average**	**Above average**
😐	🙂	😎
Attempts to demonstrate but does not show the correct technique	**Able to perform most of the technique correctly some of the time**	**Performs the technique correctly most of the time**

Assessment	😐	🙂	😎
Toes are pointed			
Kick is alternating up and down			
Legs are together			
Kick comes from the hips			

Lesson Plan #34

Lesson type: front crawl leg kick
Level: adult or child intermediate
Previous learning: basic front crawl technique
Lesson aim: to strengthen and develop front crawl leg kick
Equipment: floats, kickboards, sinkers and hoop

Exercise/Activity	Teaching Points	Organisation	Duration
Entry: swivel or sitting dive entry	enter slowly	all together	1 min
Warm up: 2 widths any stroke	take your time	all together	3 mins
Main Theme: 2 widths full stroke front crawl	kick with long legs	all together	3 mins
kicking with one float held in front	kick from the hips	all together	3 mins
push and glide	Keep legs straight and feet together	one by one	4 mins
push and glide adding leg kicks	kick with feet together	one by one	4 mins
kicking with one float held vertically in front	kick with floppy feet	all together	2 mins
2 widths full stroke front crawl	kick with relaxed legs	all together	3 mins
Contrasting Activity: surface diving through a submerged hoop	hold your breath	2 or 3 at a time	2 mins
surface diving to retrieve sinkers	relax and stay still	2 or 3 at a time	2 mins
Exit: using the pool steps	take your time	one by one	1 min

Total time: 28 minutes

Lesson #34 Assessment

Lesson Objective: to strengthen and develop front crawl leg kick		
Below average	**Average**	**Above average**
😐	🙂	😎
Attempts to demonstrate but does not show the correct technique	Able to perform most of the technique correctly some of the time	Performs the technique correctly most of the time

Assessment	😐	🙂	😎
Toes remain pointed whilst kicking			
Kick is relaxed and alternating			
Feet break the water surface			
Leg kick is rhythmical			

Lesson Plan #35

Lesson type: front crawl leg kick
Level: adult or child advanced
Previous learning: full stroke front crawl
Lesson aim: to develop and perfect front crawl leg kick
Equipment: fins and floats or kickboards

Exercise/Activity	Teaching Points	Organisation	Duration
Entry: sitting or shallow dive entry	take your time	waves	1 min
Warm up: 2 lengths any stroke	take your time	all together	3 mins
Main Theme: 1 length full stroke front crawl	kick with long legs	all together	3 mins
push and glide adding leg kicks	relaxed continuous kick	all together	3 mins
kicking with one float held vertically in front	kick with floppy feet	one by one	3 mins
vertical kicking using fins, remain upright, arms across the chest	kick from the hips	all together	3 mins
streamlined kicking using fins, arms out in front	continuous, steady kick	waves	3 mins
2 lengths full stroke front crawl	kick with relaxed legs	all together	3 mins
Contrasting Activity: push and glide into forward somersault	arms pull down to rotate	2 or 3 at a time	2 mins
supine push and glide into somersault	tuck chin to chest	2 or 3 at a time	2 mins
Exit: using the pool steps	take your time	waves	1 min

Total time: 27 minutes

Lesson #35 Assessment

Lesson Objective: to develop and perfect front crawl leg kick		
Below average	**Average**	**Above average**
😐	🙂	😎
Attempts to demonstrate but does not show the correct technique	**Able to perform most of the technique correctly some of the time**	**Performs the technique correctly most of the time**

Assessment	😐	🙂	😎
Toes break the water surface			
Knees and ankles are relaxed			
Leg kick remains relaxed when added to the whole stroke			
Leg kick is rhythmical and in time with the arm action			

Lesson Plan #36

Lesson type: front crawl arms
Level: adult or child beginner
Previous learning: basic front paddle and submerging the face
Lesson aim: to introduce basic front crawl arm action
Equipment: floats, buoyancy aids as necessary

Exercise/Activity	Teaching Points	Organisation	Duration
Entry: swivel entry	enter slowly	all together	1 min
Warm up: 2 widths any stroke using buoyancy aids	take your time	all together	3 mins
Main Theme: standing the poolside demonstrating arm action	continuous smooth action	all together	2 mins
walking through the water using arms	Keep fingers together	waves	3 mins
single arm action with float held in one hand	elbow exits first	one by one	4 mins
repeat the above with the opposite arm	finger tips enter first	one by one	4 mins
front crawl catch up holding a float	reach over the surface	waves	3 mins
full stroke front crawl	continuous arm action	all together	3 mins
Contrasting Activity: push and glide (longest distance contest)	stretched out and long body	2 or 3 at a time	2 mins
supine push and glide	push your hips up	2 or 3 at a time	2 mins
Exit: using the pool steps	take your time	one by one	1 min

Total time: 28 minutes

Lesson #36 Assessment

Lesson Objective: to introduce basic front crawl arm action		
Below average	**Average**	**Above average**
😐	🙂	😎
Attempts to demonstrate but does not show the correct technique	Able to perform most of the technique correctly some of the time	Performs the technique correctly most of the time

Assessment	😐	🙂	😎
Arm pulls are alternating			
Elbows bend with each pull			
Fingers are together			
Arms recover over the water surface			

Lesson Plan #37

Lesson type: front crawl arms
Level: adult or child intermediate
Previous learning: basic front crawl technique
Lesson aim: to progress basic front crawl arm action and introduce breathing
Equipment: floats, pull buoys and sinkers

Exercise/Activity	Teaching Points	Organisation	Duration
Entry: swivel entry	enter slowly	all together	1 min
Warm up: 2 widths full stroke front crawl	take your time	all together	3 mins
Main Theme: single arm action with float held in one hand	elbow exits first	one by one	4 mins
repeat the above with the opposite arm	finger tips enter first	one by one	4 mins
repeat single arm exercises with float, adding breathing technique	breathe to the pulling side	waves	3 mins
front crawl catch up holding a float	reach over the surface	waves	3 mins
front crawl arms only using a pull buoy	pull with power	waves	3 mins
full stroke front crawl	smooth arm action	all together	3 mins
Contrasting Activity: sitting dive	head tucked into arms	2 or 3 at a time	2 mins
surface dive and collect sinkers	head tucked down, eyes open	2 or 3 at a time	2 mins
Exit: using the pool steps	take your time	one by one	1 min

Total time: 29 minutes

Lesson #37 Assessment

Lesson Objective: to progress basic front crawl arm action and introduce breathing		
Below average	**Average**	**Above average**
😐	🙂	😎
Attempts to demonstrate but does not show the correct technique	Able to perform most of the technique correctly some of the time	Performs the technique correctly most of the time

Assessment	😐	🙂	😎
Arm pulls are relaxed and alternating			
Elbows bend and exit the water first			
Finger tips enter the water first			
Arm recovery over the water surface is relaxed and controlled			
Arm pulls are continuous as a breath is taken			

Lesson Plan #38

Lesson type: front crawl arms
Level: adult or child advanced
Previous learning: full stroke front crawl
Lesson aim: to develop and fine-tune front crawl arm action
Equipment: fins, pull buoy, hand paddles

Exercise/Activity	Teaching Points	Organisation	Duration
Entry: sitting or shallow dive entry	take your time	waves	1 min
Warm up: 2 lengths full stroke front crawl	take your time	all together	3 mins
Main Theme: front crawl arms only using a pull buoy	continuous, smooth arms	waves	3 mins
using fins, single arm pull with opposite arm stretched out in front	finger tips enter first	waves	3 mins
repeat above drill with opposite arm	stretch then pull	waves	3 mins
using fins, front crawl catch up holding a float	reach over the surface	waves	3 mins
front crawl with hand paddles	pull with power	waves	3 mins
full stroke front crawl	smooth arm action	all together	3 mins
Contrasting Activity: front crawl to poolside and somersault	plant feet onto the poolside	2 or 3 at a time	3 mins
basic front crawl start	head tucked down on entry	2 or 3 at a time	3 mins
Exit: using the pool steps or over the poolside	take your time	waves	1 min

Total time: 29 minutes

Lesson #38 Assessment

Lesson Objective: to develop and fine-tune front crawl arm action		
Below average	**Average**	**Above average**
😐	🙂	😎
Attempts to demonstrate but does not show the correct technique	Able to perform most of the technique correctly some of the time	Performs the technique correctly most of the time

Assessment	😐	🙂	😎
Arms pull under the body to the thighs			
Arm recovery is controlled and not rushed			
Hands enter inside the shoulder line and stretch forwards			
Arm recovery over the water surface is relaxed and controlled			
Elbow exists first			

Lesson Plan #39

Lesson type: front crawl breathing
Level: adult or child beginner
Previous learning: basic front paddle, submerging face and blowing bubbles
Lesson aim: to introduce basic front crawl breathing technique
Equipment: floats, buoyancy aids and sinkers as necessary

Exercise/Activity	Teaching Points	Organisation	Duration
Entry: swivel entry	enter slowly	all together	1 min
Warm up: 2 widths any stroke on the front	take your time	all together	3 mins
Main Theme: breathing while standing and holding poolside	blow slowly and gently	all together	2 mins
repeat the above, but rolling the head to the side	look to your shoulder	all together	2 mins
holding a float with a diagonal grip	blow through your mouth	waves	3 mins
single arm pull with float held in one hand	turn your head to the pulling arm	one by one	4 mins
repeat the above with the opposite arm	turn your head as your arm pulls	one by one	4 mins
full stroke front crawl	head returns to central	all together	3 mins
Contrasting Activity: head first surface dive to collect sinkers	dig yourself down to the bottom	waves	2 mins
prone star floats	take a deep breath	waves	2 mins
Exit: using the pool steps	take your time	one by one	1 min

Total time: 27 minutes

Lesson #39 Assessment

Lesson Objective: to introduce basic front crawl breathing technique		
Below average	**Average**	**Above average**
😐	🙂	😎
Attempts to demonstrate but does not show the correct technique	Able to perform most of the technique correctly some of the time	Performs the technique correctly most of the time

Assessment	😐	🙂	😎
Head is in a central position			
Head is face down			
Exhalation is from the mouth			
Head rolls to the side			
Head turns to the arm pulling side			

Lesson Plan #40

Lesson type: front crawl breathing
Level: adult or child intermediate
Previous learning: basic front crawl technique
Lesson aim: to develop and progress front crawl breathing technique
Equipment: floats and/or kickboards

Exercise/Activity	Teaching Points	Organisation	Duration
Entry: swivel or sitting dive entry	enter slowly	waves/ all together	1 min
Warm up: 2 widths any stroke	take your time	all together	3 mins
Main Theme: 2 widths full stroke front crawl	slow and steady	all together	3 mins
holding a float with a diagonal grip	breathe out slowly	waves	3 mins
single arm pull with float held in one hand	one ear up, one ear down	waves	3 mins
repeat the above with the opposite arm	look at your shoulder	waves	3 mins
repeat the above, one width each arm, breathing with alternate arm pulls	steady, controlled breathing	waves	3 mins
full stroke breathing every 3 arm pulls	take your time	waves	3 mins
Contrasting Activity: treading water	ears above the water	all together	2 mins
head first sculling	look up at the sky	waves	3 mins
Exit: using the pool steps	take your time	one by one	1 min

Total time: 28 minutes

Lesson #40 Assessment

Lesson Objective: to develop and progress basic front crawl breathing technique		
Below average	**Average**	**Above average**
😐	🙂	😎
Attempts to demonstrate but does not show the correct technique	**Able to perform most of the technique correctly some of the time**	**Performs the technique correctly most of the time**

Assessment	😐	🙂	😎
Breath is taken at regular intervals			
Head rolls to the side enough for the mouth to clear the water surface			
Exhalation is slow and controlled			
Head rolls to the side as the arm pulls			
Head rolls back down without lifting			

Lesson Plan #41

Lesson type: front crawl breathing
Level: adult or child advanced
Previous learning: full stroke front crawl
Lesson aim: to develop and perfect front crawl breathing technique
Equipment: fins, pull buoy, floats and/or kickboard

Exercise/Activity	Teaching Points	Organisation	Duration
Entry: sitting or shallow dive entry	take your time	waves	1 min
Warm up: 2 lengths front crawl	take your time	all together	3 mins
Main Theme: 1 length full stroke front crawl, breathing every 3 arm pulls	slow and steady	all together	3 mins
full stroke with pull buoy, breathing every 3 arm pulls	look at your shoulder	waves	3 mins
single arm pull with float held in one hand, increase time interval between breaths	one ear up, one ear down	waves	3 mins
repeat the above with the opposite arm	breathe out slowly	waves	3 mins
using fins, front crawl catch up increasing time interval between breaths	steady, controlled breathing	waves	3 mins
full stroke breathing every 3 arm pulls	take your time	waves	3 mins
Contrasting Activity: front crawl to the wall, somersault and push off on the back	plan feet on the pool wall	waves	3 mins
basic front crawl start	push hard from the legs	waves	3 mins
Exit: using the pool steps or over the poolside	take your time	one by one	1 min

Total time: 29 minutes

Lesson #41 Assessment

Lesson Objective: to develop and perfect front crawl breathing technique		
Below average	**Average**	**Above average**
😐	🙂	😎
Attempts to demonstrate but does not show the correct technique	**Able to perform most of the technique correctly some of the time**	**Performs the technique correctly most of the time**

Assessment	😐	🙂	😎
Breathing is bi-lateral*			
Head remains level when rolling to the side			
Exhalation is slow and controlled			
Inhalation takes place in time with the arm pull			
Head rolls back down in time with arm recovery			
Breathing takes place at regular intervals			

*bi-lateral breathing is not compulsory. Breathing only to one side may be preferred when swimming longer distances.

Lesson Plan #42

Lesson type: front crawl timing and coordination

Level: adult or child beginner
Previous learning: basic front paddle with submerging face
Lesson aim: to introduce a basic front crawl timing pattern
Equipment: floats, buoyancy aids and sinkers as necessary

Exercise/Activity	Teaching Points	Organisation	Duration
Entry: swivel entry	enter slowly	all together	1 min
Warm up: 2 widths any stroke on the front	take your time	all together	3 mins
Main Theme: push and glide from the poolside	keep hands and feet together	one by one	3 mins
push and glide holding a float, adding leg kicks	count your kicks '1,2,3,4,5,6'	waves	3 mins
alternate arm pulls holding float out in front	Count '1,2,3' each pull	waves	3 mins
front crawl 'catch up' (repeat above without a float)	continuous leg kick	waves	3 mins
push and glide adding kicks and then arm pulls	count your kicks	one by one	4 mins
full stroke front crawl	continuous arms and legs	all together	3 mins
Contrasting Activity: supine star floats	look up at the sky and stretch out	2 or 3 at a time	2 mins
submerge to collect sinkers	deep breath and relax	2 or 3 at a time	2 mins
Exit: using the pool steps	take your time	one by one	1 min

Total time: 27 minutes

Lesson #42 Assessment

Lesson Objective: to introduce a basic front crawl timing pattern		
Below average	**Average**	**Above average**
😐	🙂	😎
Attempts to demonstrate but does not show the correct technique	Able to perform most of the technique correctly some of the time	Performs the technique correctly most of the time

Assessment	😐	🙂	😎
Leg kicks are regular and alternating			
Arm pulls are regular and alternating			
Legs continue kicking when arms are pulling			
Arms continue to pull when legs are kicking			

Lesson Plan #43

Lesson type: front crawl timing and coordination

Level: adult or child intermediate
Previous learning: basic timing technique
Lesson aim: to progress and develop previous learning of front crawl timing
Equipment: floats, pull buoys and hoop

Exercise/Activity	Teaching Points	Organisation	Duration
Entry: swivel or sitting dive entry	enter slowly	waves/ all together	1 min
Warm up: 2 widths any stroke	take your time	all together	3 mins
Main Theme: 2 widths full stroke front crawl	slow and steady	all together	2 mins
kicking holding a float in both hands	count your kicks in groups of 6	waves	3 mins
alternate arm pulls holding float out in front	count '1,2,3' each pull	waves	3 mins
arm pulls with pull buoy between the legs	continuous arms	waves	3 mins
push and glide, add arms pulls and leg kicks	continuous kicking	waves	3 mins
full stroke front crawl	let the stroke flow	waves	3 mins
Contrasting Activity: feet first surface dives through a submerged hoop	stretch up and sink	one by one	4 mins
feet first sculling	toes at the surface	waves	3 mins
Exit: using the pool steps	take your time	one by one	1 min

Total time: 29 minutes

Lesson #43 Assessment

Lesson Objective: to progress and develop previous learning of front crawl timing

Below average	Average	Above average
😐	🙂	😎
Attempts to demonstrate but does not show the correct technique	Able to perform most of the technique correctly some of the time	Performs the technique correctly most of the time

Assessment	😐	🙂	😎
Legs kick in a regular pattern, in time with the arm pulls.			
Arms pull in a regular pattern with the leg kicks			
Leg kicking pattern remains continuous			
Arm pull pattern remains continuous			

Lesson Plan #44

Lesson type: front crawl timing and coordination

Level: adult or child advanced
Previous learning: full stroke front crawl
Lesson aim: to develop and fine-tune front crawl timing
Equipment: fins and pull buoys

Exercise/Activity	Teaching Points	Organisation	Duration
Entry: sitting or shallow dive entry	take your time	waves	1 min
Warm up: 2 lengths front crawl	take your time	all together	3 mins
Main Theme: 1 length full stroke front crawl	slow and steady	all together	2 mins
using fins, swim slow motion front crawl	keep head level	waves	3 mins
using fins, steady pace front crawl	let the kicks balance the arm pulls	waves	3 mins
arm pulls with pull buoy between the legs	continuous arms	waves	3 mins
push and glide, add arms pulls and leg kicks	continuous kicking	waves	3 mins
full stroke front crawl	stay level and balanced	waves	3 mins
Contrasting Activity: swim front crawl to poolside and flip turn	twist and extend away	waves	3 mins
front crawl grab start	fast transition to stroke	waves	3 mins
Exit: using the pool steps	take your time	one by one	1 min

Total time: 28 minutes

Lesson #44 Assessment

Lesson Objective: to develop and fine-tune front crawl timing

Below average	Average	Above average
😐	🙂	😎
Attempts to demonstrate but does not show the correct technique	Able to perform most of the technique correctly some of the time	Performs the technique correctly most of the time

Assessment	😐	🙂	😎
Legs kick 6 kicks to each cycle of arm pulls			
Legs kick and arms pull in a continuous and regular pattern			
Regular timing pattern is sustained over longer distances			

Lesson Plan #45

Lesson type: full stroke breaststroke

Level: adult or child beginner
Previous learning: Child - basic front paddle Adult - none
Lesson aim: to learn the basics of breaststroke and experience the whole stroke
Equipment: floats, woggle, buoyancy aids if needed and hoop

Exercise/Activity	Teaching Points	Organisation	Duration
Entry: swivel or steps entry	enter slowly	all together	1 min
Warm up: 2 widths any stroke with buoyancy aids if needed	take your time	all together	3 mins
Main Theme: full stroke, slowly with a woggle under the arms	pull in a circle, kick in a circle	all together	2 mins
push and glide, holding floats if needed	stretch out and relax	waves	3 mins
supine kicking with woggle under arms	turn out your feet	waves	3 mins
arm pulls, walking through shallow water	keep hands underwater	waves	4 mins
arm pulls with breathing, woggle under the arms	blow your hands forwards	waves	3 mins
full stroke, with bouyancy aids if needed	pull *then* kick	waves	3 mins
Contrasting Activity: supine star float	stretch out and relax	2 or 3 at a time	3 mins
sitting dive through a hoop at the surface	head tucked down	2 or 3 at a time	3 mins
Exit: using the pool steps or over the poolside	take your time	one by one	1 min

Total time: 29 minutes

Lesson #45 Assessment

Lesson Objective: to learn each part of basic breaststroke and experience the whole stroke		
Below average	**Average**	**Above average**
😐	🙂	😎
Attempts to demonstrate but does not show the correct technique	**Able to perform most of the technique correctly some of the time**	**Performs the technique correctly most of the time**

Assessment	😐	🙂	😎
Arms pull in a circular path			
Legs kick in a circular path			
Feet attempt to turn outwards			
Exhalation takes place underwater			
Arm pull and leg kick sequence is continuous			

Lesson Plan #46

Lesson type: full stroke breaststroke
Level: adult or child intermediate
Previous learning: basic breaststroke technique
Lesson aim: to progress and develop the whole stroke to an intermediate level
Equipment: floats, sinkers and hoop

Exercise/Activity	Teaching Points	Organisation	Duration
Entry: swivel or sitting dive entry	enter slowly	waves	1 min
Warm up: 2 widths any stroke	take your time	all together	3 mins
Main Theme: 2 widths full stroke breaststroke with buoyancy aids if needed	pull in a circle, kick in a circle	waves	2 mins
push and glide from the poolside	hands and feet together	one by one	3 mins
kicking with a float under each arm	knees together and kick around	waves	3 mins
push and glide adding arm pulls	pull in small circles	waves	3 mins
kicking with a float, adding breathing	kick and blow out	waves	3 mins
full stroke without buoyancy aids	kick your hands forwards	waves	3 mins
Contrasting Activity: head first surface dives, collecting sinkers placed apart	deep breath and dig down	one by one	3 mins
dolphin kick through a hoop at the surface	swim like a mermaid	one by one	3 mins
Exit: using the pool steps or over the poolside	take your time	one by one	1 min

Total time: 28 minutes

Lesson #46 Assessment

Lesson Objective: to progress and develop the whole stroke to an intermediate level		
Below average	**Average**	**Above average**
😐	🙂	😎
Attempts to demonstrate but does not show the correct technique	Able to perform most of the technique correctly some of the time	Performs the technique correctly most of the time

Assessment	😐	🙂	😎
Arms pull in a small circle			
Legs kick in a circular path with knees close together			
Feet attempt to turn outwards			
Exhalation takes place as the legs kick around and back			
Arms pull and legs kick in an alternating sequence.			

Lesson Plan #47

Lesson type: full stroke breaststroke

Level: adult or child advanced
Previous learning: full stroke breaststroke
Lesson aim: to develop and fine-tune technique for the whole stroke
Equipment: floats

Exercise/Activity	Teaching Points	Organisation	Duration
Entry: sitting or shallow dive entry	take your time	waves	1 min
Warm up: 2 lengths any stroke	take your time	all together	3 mins
Main Theme: 2 lengths full stroke breaststroke	stretch and glide	waves	2 mins
kicking with a float held vertically	feet whip around with power	waves	3 mins
push and glide, adding arm pull into another glide	hands stay in front of shoulders	waves	3 mins
full stroke breathing alternate stroke cycles	blow your hands forwards	waves	3 mins
full stroke, 2 legs kicks to 1 arm pull	kick and glide	waves	3 mins
2 lengths full stroke breaststroke	smooth flowing movements	waves	3 mins
Contrasting Activity: dolphin kick underwater, arms by sides	lead with your head	one by one	3 mins
treading water	head above the water	waves	3 mins
Exit: using the pool steps or over the poolside	take your time	one by one	1 min

Total time: 28 minutes

Lesson #47 Assessment

Lesson Objective: to develop and fine-tune technique for the whole stroke

Below average	Average	Above average
😐	🙂	😎
Attempts to demonstrate but does not show the correct technique	Able to perform most of the technique correctly some of the time	Performs the technique correctly most of the time

Assessment	😐	🙂	😎
Arms pull in a small circle and elbows tuck in			
Legs kick in a powerful whips action with knees close together			
Feet turn out to kick and then point to glide			
Inhalation takes place as the arms pull			
Exhalation takes place as the legs kick into a glide			
pull, breathe, kick, glide' sequence is smooth and continuous			

Lesson Plan #48

Lesson type: breaststroke body position
Level: adult or child beginner
Previous learning: basic front paddle and submerging the face
Lesson aim: to learn basic breaststroke body position
Equipment: floats, woggles and sinkers

Exercise/Activity	Teaching Points	Organisation	Duration
Entry: swivel entry	enter slowly	all together	1 min
Warm up: 2 widths any stroke using buoyancy aids	take your time	all together	3 mins
Main Theme: floating holding the poolside, using buoyancy aids if needed	feel the water supporting you	all together	2 mins
floating with float held under each arm	lay flat and streamlined	all together	2 mins
push and glide with a float under each arm	face in the water	waves	4 mins
push and glide with a woggle to support	face in the water and stretch out	waves	3 mins
push and glide with arms extended	hands and feet together	waves	2 mins
full stroke breaststroke with buoyancy aids if needed	pull and kick in a circle	waves	3 mins
Contrasting Activity: submerging to collect an object	take your time	2 or 3 at a time	4 mins
tuck (mushroom) float	chin and knees to chest	all together	2 mins
Exit: using the pool steps or over the poolside	take your time	one by one	1 min

Total time: 27 minutes

Lesson #48 Assessment

Lesson Objective: to learn basic breaststroke body position		
Below average	**Average**	**Above average**
😐	🙂	😎
Attempts to demonstrate but does not show the correct technique	Able to perform most of the technique correctly some of the time	Performs the technique correctly most of the time

Assessment	😐	🙂	😎
Face is submerged			
Body position is flat			
Legs and feet are together			
Hands are together			
Hips are level			
Shoulders are level			

Lesson Plan #49

Lesson type: breaststroke body position
Level: adult or child intermediate
Previous learning: basic breaststroke breaststroke technique
Lesson aim: to improve basic breaststroke body position and shape
Equipment: floats and/or woggles and hoop

Exercise/Activity	Teaching Points	Organisation	Duration
Entry: swivel entry	enter slowly	all together	1 min
Warm up: 2 widths any stroke without using buoyancy aids	take your time	all together	3 mins
Main Theme: push and glide using buoyancy aids if needed	relax and stretch	waves	3 mins
push and glide without buoyancy aids	arm extended with face submerged	waves	3 mins
push and glide adding leg kicks, returning to a glide position	feet together when gliding	waves	3 mins
push and glide adding arm pull, returning to a glide position	hands together when gliding	waves	3 mins
push and glide adding 1 arm pull, 1 leg kick and return to glide	hands and feet together to glide	waves	3 mins
2 widths full stroke breaststroke	pull, kick and then glide	waves	3 mins
Contrasting Activity: forward somersault from a push and glide	tuck chin on chest	2 or 3 at a time	3 mins
sitting dive through a submerged hoop	hands together	2 or 3 at a time	3 mins
Exit: using the pool steps or over the poolside	take your time	one by one	1 min

Total time: 29 minutes

Lesson #49 Assessment

Lesson Objective: to improve basic breaststroke body position and shape		
Below average	**Average**	**Above average**
😐	🙂	😎
Attempts to demonstrate but does not show the correct technique	Able to perform most of the technique correctly some of the time	Performs the technique correctly most of the time

Assessment	😐	🙂	😎
Face is submerged whilst moving			
Body position is horizontal			
Feet are together whilst gliding			
Hands are together whilst gliding			
Hips remain level whilst gliding			
Shoulders remain level whilst gliding			

Lesson Plan #50

Lesson type: breaststroke body position
Level: adult or child advanced
Previous learning: full stroke breaststroke
Lesson aim: to develop and fine-tune breaststroke body position and shape
Equipment: buoyancy aids if needed

Exercise/Activity	Teaching Points	Organisation	Duration
Entry: sitting or shallow dive entry	take your time	all together	1 min
Warm up: 2 lengths any stroke	steady pace	all together	3 mins
Main Theme: 2 lengths full stroke breaststroke	let the stroke flow	all together	3 mins
push and glide with face submerged	cut through the water	waves	3 mins
push and glide adding leg kicks, counting a 2 second glide between kicks	feet together when gliding	waves	3 mins
push and glide adding arm pulls, counting a 2 second glide between pulls	hands together when gliding	waves	3 mins
full stroke with 2 legs kicks to 1 arm pull	streamlined shape when gliding	waves	3 mins
2 lengths full stroke breaststroke	pull, kick and glide	waves	3 mins
Contrasting Activity: supine push and glide and rotate to prone position	keep head level	2 or 3 at a time	3 mins
any stroke with somersault mid swim	head down, chin to chest	2 or 3 at a time	3 mins
Exit: using the pool steps or over the poolside	take your time	all together	1 min

Total time: 29 minutes

Lesson #50 Assessment

Lesson Objective: to develop and fine-tune breaststroke body position and shape		
Below average	**Average**	**Above average**
😐	🙂	😎
Attempts to demonstrate but does not show the correct technique	**Able to perform most of the technique correctly some of the time**	**Performs the technique correctly most of the time**

Assessment	😐	🙂	😎
Face is submerged and head is level			
Body position remains streamlined whilst gliding			
Feet are together with toes pointed whilst gliding			
Arms are stretched out and streamlined			
Hips and shoulders are level whilst gliding			
Head remains in a neutral position whilst gliding			

Lesson Plan #51

Lesson type: breaststroke leg kick
Level: adult or child beginner
Previous learning: basic front paddle and gliding
Lesson aim: to learn basic breaststroke leg kick
Equipment: floats or kick-boards, buoyancy aids as necessary and hoop

Exercise/Activity	Teaching Points	Organisation	Duration
Entry: swivel entry	enter slowly	all together	1 min
Warm up: 2 widths any stroke using buoyancy aids	take your time	all together	3 mins
Main Theme: sitting the poolside demonstrating kicking action	Diamond, star, crocodile snap!	all together	2 mins
full stroke with buoyancy aids	kick like a frog	all together	3 mins
kicking with a float held under each arm	kick around and together	waves	3 mins
kicking supine with a float held under each arm	turn out your feet like a penguin	waves	4 mins
kicking with one float held in front	kick and glide	waves	3 mins
full stroke with buoyancy aids if necessary	breathe, kick, glide	all together	3 mins
Contrasting Activity: supine star float	chin to chest	one by one	2 mins
push and glide through a hoop	hands and feet together	one by one	2 mins
Exit: using the pool steps	take your time	one by one	1 min

Total time: 27 minutes

Lesson #51 Assessment

Lesson Objective: to learn basic breaststroke leg kick		
Below average	**Average**	**Above average**
😐	🙂	😎
Attempts to demonstrate but does not show the correct technique	Able to perform most of the technique correctly some of the time	Performs the technique correctly most of the time

Assessment	😐	🙂	😎
Legs kick simultaneously in a circular path			
Feet turn outwards			
Feet return together			
Kick is followed by a glide			

Lesson Plan #52

Lesson type: breaststroke leg kick
Level: adult or child intermediate
Previous learning: basic breaststroke technique
Lesson aim: to strengthen and develop basic breaststroke leg kick
Equipment: floats, buoyancy aids and hoop

Exercise/Activity	Teaching Points	Organisation	Duration
Entry: swivel or sitting dive entry	enter slowly	all together	1 min
Warm up: 2 widths full stroke breaststroke	take your time	all together	3 mins
Main Theme: supine leg kick with woggle or floats	kick and glide	all together	2 mins
kicking with a float held under each arm	snap feet together	waves	3 mins
kicking with one float held in front	kick with power	waves	3 mins
kicking with one float held in front adding a glide	feet together when gliding	waves	3 mins
kick with floats held under each arm plus breaths	kick and blow	waves	3 mins
2 widths full stroke breaststroke	breathe, kick, glide	all together	3 mins
Contrasting Activity: sitting dives	chin to chest	one by one	3 mins
push and glide through a submerged hoop	hands and feet together	one by one	3 mins
Exit: using the pool steps	take your time	one by one	1 min

Total time: 28 minutes

Lesson #52 Assessment

Lesson Objective: to strengthen and develop basic breaststroke leg kick		
Below average	**Average**	**Above average**
😐	🙂	😎
Attempts to demonstrate but does not show the correct technique	Able to perform most of the technique correctly some of the time	Performs the technique correctly most of the time

Assessment	😐	🙂	😎
Legs kick simultaneously with power			
Feet turn outwards			
Feet return together with toes pointed			
Kick is followed by a streamlined glide			

Lesson Plan #53

Lesson type: breaststroke leg kick
Level: adult or child advanced
Previous learning: full stroke breaststroke
Lesson aim: to develop and perfect breaststroke leg kick
Equipment: floats or kickboards

Exercise/Activity	Teaching Points	Organisation	Duration
Entry: sitting or shallow dive entry	take your time	waves	1 min
Warm up: 2 lengths any stroke	take your time	all together	3 mins
Main Theme: 2 lengths full stroke breaststroke	smooth flowing movements	all together	3 mins
leg kicks with a float held vertically	whip your feet around	waves	3 mins
kicking with a float held in front, counting leg kicks	kick and glide	one by one	3 mins
kicking with arms extended, counting leg kicks	feet whip together	waves	3 mins
kicking vertically (treading water) in deep water	push with your heels	all together	3 mins
2 lengths full stroke breaststroke	kick into a glide	all together	3 mins
Contrasting Activity: push and glide into forward somersault	arms pull down to rotate	2 or 3 at a time	2 mins
supine push and glide into somersault	tuck chin to chest	2 or 3 at a time	2 mins
Exit: using the pool steps	take your time	waves	1 min

Total time: 27 minutes

Lesson #53 Assessment

Lesson Objective: to develop and perfect breaststroke leg kick		
Below average	**Average**	**Above average**
😐	🙂	😎
Attempts to demonstrate but does not show the correct technique	Able to perform most of the technique correctly some of the time	Performs the technique correctly most of the time

Assessment	😐	🙂	😎
Legs kick simultaneously with power			
Feet turn outwards and then whip around			
Feet return together with toes pointed			
Kick is followed by a streamlined glide			

Lesson Plan #54

Lesson type: breaststroke arms
Level: adult or child beginner
Previous learning: basic breaststroke technique
Lesson aim: to learn and practice basic breaststroke arm pull
Equipment: floats, woggles, buoyancy aids as necessary and hoop

Exercise/Activity	Teaching Points	Organisation	Duration
Entry: swivel entry	hold the side with both hands	all together	1 min
Warm up: 2 widths any stroke with buoyancy aids	take your time	all together	3 mins
Main Theme: 2 widths full stroke breaststroke	pull in a circle and kick in a circle	all together	3 mins
sitting on the poolside demonstrating arm action	scoop around in a circle shape	all together	3 mins
walking though the water using arm action	pull the water apart	all together	3 mins
arm action with a woggle under the arms	pull in a *small* circle	all together	3 mins
arms and legs with woggle under the arms	stretch arms out front	all together	3 mins
full stroke with buoyancy aids if necessary	pull around and stretch	all together	3 mins
Contrasting Activity: supine star float	look up and relax	one by one	3 mins
swimming through a partially submerged hoop	eyes open	one by one	3 mins
Exit: using the pool steps or over the poolside	take your time	one by one	1 min

Total time: 29 minutes

Lesson #54 Assessment

Lesson Objective: to learn and practice basic breaststroke arm pull		
Below average	**Average**	**Above average**
😐	🙂	😎
Attempts to demonstrate but does not show the correct technique	Able to perform most of the technique correctly some of the time	Performs the technique correctly most of the time

Assessment	😐	🙂	😎
Arm pulls are simultaneous			
Elbows bend and tuck in			
Fingers are together			
Arms stretch forwards			

Lesson Plan #55

Lesson type: breaststroke arms
Level: adult or child intermediate
Previous learning: basic breaststroke technique
Lesson aim: to develop and progress breaststroke arm technique
Equipment: floats and/or woggles and sinkers

Exercise/Activity	Teaching Points	Organisation	Duration
Entry: swivel entry or sitting dive entry	take your time	all together	1 min
Warm up: 2 widths any stroke	continuous swimming	all together	2 mins
Main Theme: 2 widths full stroke breaststroke	pull in a circle and kick in a circle	all together	3 mins
arm action with a woggle under the arms	fingers together	waves	3 mins
arms pulls with woggle under the arms, adding breathing	stretch forwards	waves	3 mins
push and glide adding arm pulls	pull in a *small* circle	waves	3 mins
push and glide adding alternate arm pull, leg kick action in slow motion	keep hands in front of the shoulders	all together	3 mins
full stroke breaststroke	hands together when gliding	all together	3 mins
Contrasting Activity: treading water	mouth and nose out of the water	one by one	2 mins
retrieve an object from the pool floor and return it to the poolside	eyes open	one by one	4 mins
Exit: using the pool steps or over the poolside	take your time	one by one	1 min

Total time: 28 minutes

Lesson #55 Assessment

Lesson Objective: to progress basic breaststroke arm technique		
Below average	**Average**	**Above average**
😐	🙂	😎
Attempts to demonstrate but does not show the correct technique	Able to perform most of the technique correctly some of the time	Performs the technique correctly most of the time

Assessment	😐	🙂	😎
Arms pull in a small circle			
Elbows bend and tuck in			
Fingers are together			
Arms stretch forwards into a glide			

Lesson Plan #56

Lesson type: breaststroke arms
Level: adult or child advanced
Previous learning: full stroke breaststroke
Lesson aim: to develop and fine-tune breaststroke arm action
Equipment: hand paddles

Exercise/Activity	Teaching Points	Organisation	Duration
Entry: sitting or shallow dive entry	take your time	waves	1 min
Warm up: 2 lengths any stroke	take your time	all together	3 mins
Main Theme: 2 lengths full stroke breaststroke	let your movements flow	waves	3 mins
push and glide adding arm pulls	hands in front of shoulders	waves	3 mins
push and glide adding arm pulls, with hand paddles	tuck your elbows in and stretch	waves	3 mins
full stroke with hand paddles	pull with power	waves	3 mins
1 length full stroke counting strokes	pull and stretch	waves	3 mins
2 lengths full stroke breaststroke	pull, breathe, kick, glide	waves	3 mins
Contrasting Activity: feet first sculling	feet remain at the surface	waves	3 mins
basic racing start	head tucked down on entry	one at a time	3 mins
Exit: using the pool steps or over the poolside	take your time	waves	1 min

Total time: 29 minutes

Lesson #56 Assessment

Lesson Objective: to develop and fine-tune breaststroke arm action		
Below average	**Average**	**Above average**
🙂	🙂	😎
Attempts to demonstrate but does not show the correct technique	Able to perform most of the technique correctly some of the time	Performs the technique correctly most of the time

Assessment	🙂	🙂	😎
Arms pull in a small circle			
Elbows bend and tuck in			
Fingers are together throughout			
Hands remain in front of the shoulders			
Arms stretch forwards into a glide			

Lesson Plan #57

Lesson type: breaststroke breathing
Level: adult or child beginner
Previous learning: basic front paddle and submerging
Lesson aim: to learn basic breaststroke breathing technique
Equipment: floats, woggles and buoyancy aids as necessary

Exercise/Activity	Teaching Points	Organisation	Duration
Entry: pool steps or swivel entry	enter slowly	all together	1 min
Warm up: 2 widths any stroke using buoyancy aids	take your time	all together	2 mins
Main Theme: standing in water, breathing with arm action	breathe through your mouth	all together	2 mins
walking through the water using arms and breathing	blow your hands forwards	waves	3 mins
woggle held under the arms with arm pulls with breathing	face up as you breathe in	waves	3 mins
floats under each arm, kick and breathe out	face down as you breathe out	waves	4 mins
woggle under the arms, full stroke performed slowly with breathing	pull your head up, kick your head down	all together	3 mins
full stroke with breathing (use buoyancy aids if necessary)	breathe out into a glide	all together	3 mins
Contrasting Activity: pencil jump	jump away from the side	all together	2 mins
tuck float (timed)	deep breath, chin to chest	all together	2 mins
Exit: using the pool steps	take your time	one by one	1 min

Total time: 26 minutes

Lesson #57 Assessment

Lesson Objective: to learn basic breaststroke breathing technique		
Below average	**Average**	**Above average**
😐	🙂	😎
Attempts to demonstrate but does not show the correct technique	Able to perform most of the technique correctly some of the time	Performs the technique correctly most of the time

Assessment	😐	🙂	😎
Head is in a central position			
Face up to inhale			
Face down to exhale			
Breathing takes place through the mouth			

Lesson Plan #58

Lesson type: breaststroke breathing
Level: adult or child intermediate
Previous learning: basic breaststroke technique
Lesson aim: to develop and progress breaststroke breathing technique
Equipment: floats and woggles

Exercise/Activity	Teaching Points	Organisation	Duration
Entry: swivel or sitting dive entry	enter slowly	waves/ all together	1 min
Warm up: 2 widths any stroke	take your time	all together	3 mins
Main Theme: full stroke with breathing (use buoyancy aids if necessary)	breathe through your mouth	all together	3 mins
arms pulls with a woggle	blow your hands forwards	waves	3 mins
woggle under the arms, full stroke performed slowly with breathing	pull, breathe, kick, blow	waves	3 mins
1 float held in front, kick and breathe out	kick and blow	waves	3 mins
push and glide, adding 'pull, breathe, kick, blow' sequence	kick and blow your hands forwards	waves	3 mins
2 widths full stroke breaststroke	breathe out as you glide	waves	3 mins
Contrasting Activity: treading water	ears above the water	all together	2 mins
head first sculling	look up at the sky	waves	3 mins
Exit: using the pool steps	take your time	one by one	1 min

Total time: 28 minutes

Lesson #58 Assessment

Lesson Objective: to develop and progress basic breaststroke breathing technique		
Below average	**Average**	**Above average**
😐	🙂	😎
Attempts to demonstrate but does not show the correct technique	**Able to perform most of the technique correctly some of the time**	**Performs the technique correctly most of the time**

Assessment	😐	🙂	😎
Head is in a central position			
Inhale as the arms pull			
Exhale as the legs kick			
Breathing takes place through the mouth			
Exhalation continues through the glide			

Lesson Plan #59

Lesson type: breaststroke breathing
Level: adult or child advanced
Previous learning: full stroke breaststroke
Lesson aim: to develop and perfect breaststroke breathing technique
Equipment: floats and/or kickboards if needed

Exercise/Activity	Teaching Points	Organisation	Duration
Entry: sitting or shallow dive entry	take your time	waves	1 min
Warm up: 2 lengths any stroke	take your time	all together	3 mins
Main Theme: 2 lengths full stroke breaststroke	let the stroke movements flow	all together	3 mins
1 length full stroke, counting strokes	breathe out into the glide	waves	3 mins
1 length, 2 stroke cycles per breath	breathe out slowly	waves	3 mins
repeat previous drill, try to reduce the number of stroke cycles	control your breath out	waves	3 mins
1 length full stroke against the clock, using head movement to gain momentum	breathe out with power	waves	3 mins
2 lengths full stroke breaststroke	breathe out, glide and stretch	waves	3 mins
Contrasting Activity: treading water - vary with 1 arm behind the back or above the water	ears and mouth above the surface	waves	3 mins
basic racing start	push hard from the legs	waves	3 mins
Exit: using the pool steps or over the poolside	take your time	one by one	1 min

Total time: 29 minutes

Lesson #59 Assessment

Lesson Objective: to develop and perfect breaststroke breathing technique		
Below average	**Average**	**Above average**
😐	🙂	😎
Attempts to demonstrate but does not show the correct technique	**Able to perform most of the technique correctly some of the time**	**Performs the technique correctly most of the time**

Assessment	😐	🙂	😎
Head is in a central position			
Inhale as the arms pull			
Exhale as the legs kick			
Breathing takes place through the mouth			
Exhalation is continuous and unlabored			
Head dive is used to gain momentum			

Lesson Plan #60

Lesson type: breaststroke timing and coordination
Level: adult or child beginners
Previous learning: basic breaststroke arm pull and leg kick
Lesson aim: to learn basic breaststroke timing and coordination
Equipment: floats, buoyancy aids and sinkers

Exercise/Activity	Teaching Points	Organisation	Duration
Entry: swivel entry or use pool steps	enter slowly	all together	1 min
Warm up: 2 widths full stroke breaststroke, with aids if needed	pull then kick	all together	3 mins
Main Theme: Push and glide with a streamlined shape	hands together	all together	2 mins
Push and glide, adding leg kicks	kick and glide	waves	3 mins
Push and glide adding arm pulls	Pull around and stretch forward	waves	3 mins
Push and glide adding arm pulls and leg kicks	pull, kick and glide	waves	3 mins
Repeat previous exercise, adding breathing	pull, breathe and kick	waves	3 mins
Full stroke breaststroke, swum slowly	pull, breathe, kick, glide	one by one	4 mins
Contrasting Activity: pencil jump	jump away from the poolside	one by one	2 mins
retrieve sinkers	deep breath and dig deep	one by one	3 mins
Exit: Using the pool steps	take your time	one by one	1 min

Total time: 28 minutes

Lesson #60 Assessment

Lesson Objective: to learn basic breaststroke timing and coordination		
Below average	**Average**	**Above average**
😐	🙂	😎
Attempts to demonstrate but does not show the correct technique	Able to perform most of the technique correctly some of the time	Performs the technique correctly most of the time

Assessment	😐	🙂	😎
Leg kicks are simultaneous and circular			
Arm pulls are simultaneous and circular			
Pull *then* kick			
Glide after each kick			

Lesson Plan #61

Lesson type: breaststroke timing and coordination

Level: adult or child intermediate
Previous learning: basic timing technique
Lesson aim: to progress and develop previous learning of breaststroke timing
Equipment: floats if needed and hoop

Exercise/Activity	Teaching Points	Organisation	Duration
Entry: swivel or sitting dive entry	enter slowly	waves/ all together	1 min
Warm up: 2 widths any stroke	take your time	all together	3 mins
Main Theme: 2 widths full stroke breaststroke	swim with smooth movements	all together	2 mins
Push and glide with a streamlined shape	stretch and glide	waves	3 mins
push and glide, adding arm pulls and leg kicks	pull then kick	waves	3 mins
repeat previous drill, adding breaths	pull, breath, kick	waves	3 mins
push and glide, adding the stroke sequence and returning to a glide	kick into a glide	waves	3 mins
1 length full stroke breaststroke	pull, breathe, kick and glide	waves	3 mins
Contrasting Activity: feet first surface dives through a submerged hoop	stretch up and sink	one by one	4 mins
feet first sculling	toes at the surface	waves	3 mins
Exit: using the pool steps	take your time	one by one	1 min

Total time: 29 minutes

Lesson #61 Assessment

Lesson Objective: to progress and develop previous learning of breaststroke timing		
Below average	**Average**	**Above average**
😐	🙂	😎
Attempts to demonstrate but does not show the correct technique	Able to perform most of the technique correctly some of the time	Performs the technique correctly most of the time

Assessment	😐	🙂	😎
Arm pulls are followed by a breath			
Legs kick into a glide			
Pull *then* kick			
Glide after each kick			

Lesson Plan #62

Lesson type: breaststroke timing and coordination
Level: adult or child advanced
Previous learning: full stroke breaststroke
Lesson aim: to develop and fine-tune breaststroke timing
Equipment: floats and sinkers if needed

Exercise/Activity	Teaching Points	Organisation	Duration
Entry: sitting or shallow dive entry	take your time	waves	1 min
Warm up: 2 lengths any stroke	take your time	all together	3 mins
Main Theme: 2 lengths full stroke breaststroke	smooth flowing stroke	all together	2 mins
full stroke, 2 leg kicks to 1 arm pull	kick and glide	waves	3 mins
1 length counting stroke cycles	kick into the glide	one by one	3 mins
1 length counting stroke cycles, reduce the number of cycles per length	maximise your glide	one by one	3 mins
2 lengths full stroke maintaining the reduced stroke rate from previous	smooth strokes and glide	waves	3 mins
2 lengths full stroke breaststroke	pull, breathe, kick and glide	waves	3 mins
Contrasting Activity: head first surface dive and swim underwater for a pre-set distance	deep breath and dig down deep	one by one	3 mins
basic grab start	fast transition to stroke	waves	3 mins
Exit: using the pool steps	take your time	one by one	1 min

Total time: 28 minutes

Lesson #62 Assessment

Lesson Objective: to develop and fine-tune breaststroke timing		
Below average	**Average**	**Above average**
😐	🙂	😎
Attempts to demonstrate but does not show the correct technique	Able to perform most of the technique correctly some of the time	Performs the technique correctly most of the time

Assessment	😐	🙂	😎
Kick into a glide			
Pull *then* kick			
Glide after each kick			
Attempts to maximise the glide			
Reduce or maintain stroke rate			

Lesson Plan #63

Lesson type: full stroke backstroke
Level: adult or child beginner
Previous learning: basic alternating kicking and supine floating
Lesson aim: to learn the basics of backstroke and experience the whole stroke
Equipment: floats, woggle, buoyancy aids if needed and hoop

Exercise/Activity	Teaching Points	Organisation	Duration
Entry: swivel or steps entry	enter slowly	all together	1 min
Warm up: 2 widths any stroke with buoyancy aids if needed	take your time	all together	3 mins
Main Theme: kicking supine with a woggle under the arms	relax and kick	all together	2 mins
supine push and glide, holding floats if needed	hips up and stretch	waves	3 mins
supine kicking with a float held on the chest	kick with pointed toes	waves	3 mins
single arm pulls with a float held on the chest	arm stretches up and back	waves	3 mins
single arm pulls using the opposite arm with a float held on the chest	fingers together	waves	3 mins
2 widths full stroke backstroke	kick and pull continuously	waves	3 mins
Contrasting Activity: prone star float	deep breath and relax	2 or 3 at a time	3 mins
sitting dive through a hoop at the surface	head tucked down	2 or 3 at a time	3 mins
Exit: using the pool steps or over the poolside	take your time	one by one	1 min

Total time: 28 minutes

Lesson #63 Assessment

Lesson Objective: to learn the basics of backstroke and experience the whole stroke

Below average	Average	Above average
😐	🙂	😎
Attempts to demonstrate but does not show the correct technique	Able to perform most of the technique correctly some of the time	Performs the technique correctly most of the time

Assessment	😐	🙂	😎
Head is facing upwards			
Hips are at or near the surface			
Legs kick alternately			
Toes are pointed			
Arm pulls are continuous			

Lesson Plan #64

Lesson type: full stroke backstroke
Level: adult or child intermediate
Previous learning: basic backstroke technique
Lesson aim: to progress and develop the whole stroke to an intermediate level
Equipment: floats, pull buoy, sinkers and hoop

Exercise/Activity	Teaching Points	Organisation	Duration
Entry: swivel or sitting dive entry	enter slowly	waves	1 min
Warm up: 2 widths any stroke	take your time	all together	3 mins
Main Theme: 2 widths full stroke backstroke with buoyancy aids if needed	pull and kick continuously	waves	2 mins
supine push and glide from the poolside	head back, looking upwards	one by one	3 mins
supine kicking with a float behind the head	kick with floppy feet	waves	3 mins
arm pulls with a pull buoy	pull through to your thighs	waves	3 mins
arm pulls with a pull buoy, adding breathing	pull and blow	waves	3 mins
full stroke backstroke without buoyancy aids	kick your hands forwards	waves	3 mins
Contrasting Activity: head first surface dives, collecting sinkers placed apart	deep breath and dig down	one by one	3 mins
dolphin kick through a hoop at the surface	swim like a mermaid	one by one	3 mins
Exit: using the pool steps or over the poolside	take your time	one by one	1 min

Total time: 28 minutes

Lesson #64 Assessment

Lesson Objective: to progress and develop the whole stroke to an intermediate level		
Below average	**Average**	**Above average**
😐	🙂	😎
Attempts to demonstrate but does not show the correct technique	Able to perform most of the technique correctly some of the time	Performs the technique correctly most of the time

Assessment	😐	🙂	😎
Head is facing upwards with ears in the water			
Hips and tummy are at water surface			
Legs kick alternately with relaxed ankles			
Toes are pointed			
Arms pull through to the thighs			

Lesson Plan #65

Lesson type: full stroke backstroke
Level: adult or child advanced
Previous learning: full stroke backstroke
Lesson aim: to develop and fine-tune whole stroke technique
Equipment: floats

Exercise/Activity	Teaching Points	Organisation	Duration
Entry: sitting or shallow dive entry	take your time	waves	1 min
Warm up: 2 lengths any stroke	take your time	all together	3 mins
Main Theme: 2 lengths full stroke backstroke	stretch and glide	waves	2 mins
supine push and glide with arms extended	hands together and stretch	waves	3 mins
supine kicking with arms extended	kick from the hips	waves	3 mins
single arm pulls using a lane rope to help simulate bent arm pull technique	pull through your body line	waves	3 mins
full stroke using bent arm pull action	one arm pulls as the other recovers	waves	3 mins
2 lengths full stroke backstroke	continuous flowing strokes	waves	3 mins
Contrasting Activity: dolphin kick underwater, arms by sides	lead with your head	waves	3 mins
treading water	head above the water	waves	3 mins
Exit: using the pool steps or over the poolside	take your time	one by one	1 min

Total time: 28 minutes

Lesson #65 Assessment

Lesson Objective: to develop and fine-tune whole stroke technique		
Below average	**Average**	**Above average**
😐	🙂	😎
Attempts to demonstrate but does not show the correct technique	Able to perform most of the technique correctly some of the time	Performs the technique correctly most of the time

Assessment	😐	🙂	😎
Body position is flat and streamlined			
Head is back with ears in the water			
Leg kicks are relaxed and from the hips			
Ankles are relaxed with toes pointed			
One arm pulls as the other recovers			
Stroke movements are continuous and flowing			

Lesson Plan #66

Lesson type: backstroke body position
Level: adult or child beginner
Previous learning: basic back paddle and supine floating
Lesson aim: to learn basic backstroke body position
Equipment: floats, buoyancy aids and sinkers as necessary

Exercise/Activity	Teaching Points	Organisation	Duration
Entry: swivel entry	enter slowly	all together	1 min
Warm up: 2 widths any stroke using buoyancy aids	slow and gentle swim	all together	3 mins
Main Theme: static floating with a float under each arm	relax and keep still	all together	2 mins
static floating with one float held on the chest	keeps your hips up	all together	2 mins
supine push and glide, holding a float	push hips to the surface	one by one	3 mins
push and glide with a float, adding leg kicks	relax and stretch	waves	3 mins
push and glide without buoyancy aids	push off like a rocket	waves	3 mins
push and glide adding kicking and any arm action to support (eg sculling)	look upwards and keep your body flat	waves	3 mins
Contrasting Activity: submerging to collect an object	take your time	2 or 3 at a time	3 mins
submerging to collect objects placed apart	deep breath and relax	2 or 3 at a time	3 mins
Exit: using the pool steps or over the poolside	take your time	one by one	1 min

Total time: 27 minutes

Lesson #66 Assessment

Lesson Objective: to learn basic backstroke body position		
Below average	**Average**	**Above average**
😐	🙂	😎
Attempts to demonstrate but does not show the correct technique	Able to perform most of the technique correctly some of the time	Performs the technique correctly most of the time

Assessment	😐	🙂	😎
Face is looking upwards			
Body position is flat			
Legs and feet are together			
Hands are at the sides			
Hips are level			
Shoulders are level			

Lesson Plan #67

Lesson type: backstroke body position
Level: adult or child intermediate
Previous learning: basic backstroke backstroke technique
Lesson aim: to improve basic backstroke body position and shape
Equipment: floats and/or woggles and hoop

Exercise/Activity	Teaching Points	Organisation	Duration
Entry: swivel entry	enter slowly	all together	1 min
Warm up: 2 widths any stroke without using buoyancy aids	take your time	all together	3 mins
Main Theme: 2 widths full stroke backstroke	continuous arms and legs	waves	3 mins
supine push and glide, with a float if needed	push hips to the surface	waves	3 mins
push and glide without buoyancy aids	push off like a rocket	waves	3 mins
push and glide with arms extended	streamlined shape hands together	waves	3 mins
push and glide with arms extended, adding leg kicks	keep your body flat and stretched	waves	3 mins
2 widths full stroke backstroke	continuous arms and legs	waves	3 mins
Contrasting Activity: forward somersault from a push and glide	tuck chin on chest	2 or 3 at a time	3 mins
sitting dive through a submerged hoop	hands together	2 or 3 at a time	3 mins
Exit: using the pool steps or over the poolside	take your time	one by one	1 min

Total time: 29 minutes

144

Lesson #67 Assessment

Lesson Objective: to improve basic backstroke body position and shape		
Below average	**Average**	**Above average**
😐	🙂	😎
Attempts to demonstrate but does not show the correct technique	**Able to perform most of the technique correctly some of the time**	**Performs the technique correctly most of the time**

Assessment	😐	🙂	😎
Face is looking upwards with ears in the water			
Body position is flat and streamlined			
Legs and feet are together			
Hands are together when extended above the head			
Hips and shoulders are level			

Lesson Plan #68

Lesson type: backstroke body position
Level: adult or child advanced
Previous learning: full stroke backstroke
Lesson aim: to develop and fine-tune backstroke body position and shape
Equipment: buoyancy aids if needed

Exercise/Activity	Teaching Points	Organisation	Duration
Entry: sitting or shallow dive entry	take your time	all together	1 min
Warm up: 2 lengths any stroke	steady pace	all together	3 mins
Main Theme: 2 lengths full stroke backstroke	let the stroke flow	all together	3 mins
push and glide with arms extended	streamlined shape hands together	waves	3 mins
push and glide with arms extended, adding leg kicks	keep your body flat and stretched	waves	3 mins
push and glide with arms extended, adding arm pulls	stretch arms up to maintain streamlined shape	waves	3 mins
supine push and glide to submerge and kick underwater for distance	streamlined shape underwater	waves	3 mins
2 lengths full stroke backstroke from racing start	flat and level body position	waves	3 mins
Contrasting Activity: prone push and glide and rotate to supine position	keep head level	2 or 3 at a time	3 mins
any stroke with somersault mid swim	head down, chin to chest	2 or 3 at a time	3 mins
Exit: using the pool steps or over the poolside	take your time	all together	1 min

Total time: 29 minutes

Lesson #68 Assessment

Lesson Objective: to develop and fine-tune backstroke body position and shape		
Below average	**Average**	**Above average**
😐	🙂	😎
Attempts to demonstrate but does not show the correct technique	Able to perform most of the technique correctly some of the time	Performs the technique correctly most of the time

Assessment	😐	🙂	😎
Face is looking upwards with ears in the water			
Body position is flat and streamlined whilst kicking and pulling			
Legs and feet are together			
Hands are together when extended above the head			
Hips and shoulders are level when gliding			
Head remains in a neutral position whilst gliding			

Lesson Plan #69

Lesson type: backstroke leg kick
Level: adult or child beginner
Previous learning: basic back paddle
Lesson aim: to learn basic backstroke kicking action
Equipment: floats, buoyancy aids, sinkers and hoop

Exercise/Activity	Teaching Points	Organisation	Duration
Entry: swivel entry	enter slowly	all together	1 min
Warm up: 2 widths any stroke using buoyancy aids	slow and gentle swim	all together	3 mins
Main Theme: sitting on poolside, kicking legs	kick from your hips	all together	2 mins
kicking with woggle under arms	kick with floppy feet	waves	3 mins
kicking with a float held behind the head	push hips to the surface	waves	3 mins
kicking with a float held on the chest	kick with straight legs	waves	3 mins
push and glide, adding leg kicks	pointed toes	waves	3 mins
full stroke backstroke	continuous leg kick	waves	3 mins
Contrasting Activity: jump in and swim through a hoop	jump away from the side	one by one	3 mins
submerging to collect an object	deep breath and relax	2 or 3 at a time	3 mins
Exit: using the pool steps or over the poolside	take your time	one by one	1 min

Total time: 28 minutes

Lesson #69 Assessment

Lesson Objective: to learn basic backstroke leg kicking action		
Below average	**Average**	**Above average**
😐	🙂	😎
Attempts to demonstrate but does not show the correct technique	Able to perform most of the technique correctly some of the time	Performs the technique correctly most of the time

Assessment	😐	🙂	😎
Legs kicks are alternating			
Legs are straight and together			
Kick comes from the hips			
Toes are pointed			

Lesson Plan #70

Lesson type: backstroke leg kick
Level: adult or child intermediate
Previous learning: basic backstroke technique
Lesson aim: to strengthen and develop basic backstroke leg kick
Equipment: floats, buoyancy aids and hoop

Exercise/Activity	Teaching Points	Organisation	Duration
Entry: swivel or sitting dive entry	enter slowly	all together	1 min
Warm up: 2 widths any stroke	take your time	all together	3 mins
Main Theme: kicking with a float held under each arm	toes pointed	all together	2 mins
kicking with a float held behind the head	kick from the hips	waves	3 mins
kicking with one float held on the chest	kick with floppy feet	waves	3 mins
kicking with one float held, arms extended	kick with long legs	waves	3 mins
push and glide adding leg kicks	toes make a small splash	waves	3 mins
2 widths full stroke backstroke	relaxed, flowing kicks	waves	3 mins
Contrasting Activity: sitting dives	chin to chest	one by one	3 mins
push and glide through a submerged hoop	hands and feet together	one by one	3 mins
Exit: using the pool steps	take your time	one by one	1 min

Total time: 28 minutes

Lesson #70 Assessment

Lesson Objective: to strengthen and develop basic backstroke leg kick		
Below average	**Average**	**Above average**
😐	🙂	😎
Attempts to demonstrate but does not show the correct technique	Able to perform most of the technique correctly some of the time	Performs the technique correctly most of the time

Assessment	😐	🙂	😎
Legs kicks are continuous and alternating			
Legs are straight and together			
Kick comes from the hips			
Toes are pointed and ankles relaxed			

Lesson Plan #71

Lesson type: backstroke leg kick
Level: adult or child advanced
Previous learning: full stroke backstroke
Lesson aim: to develop and perfect backstroke leg kick
Equipment: floats or kickboards, fins

Exercise/Activity	Teaching Points	Organisation	Duration
Entry: sitting or shallow dive entry	take your time	waves	1 min
Warm up: 2 lengths any stroke	take your time	all together	3 mins
Main Theme: 2 lengths full stroke backstroke	smooth flowing movements	waves	3 mins
kicking with a float held behind the head (position the float to increase resistance)	kick from the hips	waves	3 mins
kicking with one float held, arms extended	kick with long legs	waves	3 mins
push and glide with arms extended, adding leg kicks	toes make a small splash	waves	3 mins
Repeat any of the above drills using fins	relaxed, flowing kicks	waves	3 mins
2 lengths full stroke backstroke	smooth flowing movements	waves	3 mins
Contrasting Activity: push and glide into forward somersault	arms pull down to rotate	2 or 3 at a time	2 mins
supine push and glide into somersault	tuck chin to chest	2 or 3 at a time	2 mins
Exit: using the pool steps	take your time	waves	1 min

Total time: 27 minutes

Lesson #71 Assessment

Lesson Objective: to develop and perfect backstroke leg kick		
Below average	**Average**	**Above average**
😐	🙂	😎
Attempts to demonstrate but does not show the correct technique	Able to perform most of the technique correctly some of the time	Performs the technique correctly most of the time

Assessment	😐	🙂	😎
Legs kicks are continuous and alternating			
Legs are straight and together			
Kick comes from the hips			
Toes are pointed and ankles relaxed			

Lesson Plan #72

Lesson type: backstroke arms
Level: adult or child beginner
Previous learning: basic back paddle
Lesson aim: to learn basic backstroke arm action
Equipment: floats, buoyancy aids and sinkers as necessary

Exercise/Activity	Teaching Points	Organisation	Duration
Entry: swivel entry	enter slowly	all together	1 min
Warm up: 2 widths any stroke using buoyancy aids	slow and gentle swim	all together	3 mins
Main Theme: standing on poolside, practice arm action	stretch up tall	all together	2 mins
single arm pull with float held on the chest	arm brushes your ear	waves	3 mins
repeat above exercise with the opposite arm	pull down to your side	waves	3 mins
single arm pull with one arm held by the side	thumb exists first	waves	3 mins
repeat above exercise with the opposite arm	little finger enters first	waves	3 mins
full stroke backstroke	continuous arm pull	waves	3 mins
Contrasting Activity: prone star float	deep breath and relax	2 or 3 at a time	3 mins
submerging to collect an object	deep breath and reach down	2 or 3 at a time	3 mins
Exit: using the pool steps or over the poolside	take your time	one by one/all together	1 min

Total time: 28 minutes

Lesson #72 Assessment

Lesson Objective: to learn and practice basic backstroke arm action		
Below average	**Average**	**Above average**
😐	🙂	😎
Attempts to demonstrate but does not show the correct technique	Able to perform most of the technique correctly some of the time	Performs the technique correctly most of the time

Assessment	😐	🙂	😎
Arm pulls are continuous			
Hand enters the water little finger first			
Fingers are together			
Arms are straight on entry			

Lesson Plan #73

Lesson type: backstroke arms
Level: adult or child intermediate
Previous learning: basic backstroke technique
Lesson aim: to develop and progress backstroke arm technique
Equipment: floats and/or woggles and sinkers

Exercise/Activity	Teaching Points	Organisation	Duration
Entry: swivel entry or sitting dive entry	take your time	all together	1 min
Warm up: 2 widths any stroke	continuous swimming	all together	2 mins
Main Theme: 2 widths full stroke backstroke	relaxed, smooth movements	all together	3 mins
arm action with a float held on the chest. Opposite arm on return width	fingers together	waves	3 mins
single arm pull with one arm held by the side	thumb exists first	waves	3 mins
repeat above exercise with the opposite arm	little finger enters first	waves	3 mins
alternating arm pulls with a pull buoy held between the legs	one arm pulls and the other recovers	all together	3 mins
full stroke backstroke	smooth flowing movements	all together	3 mins
Contrasting Activity: treading water	mouth and nose out of the water	one by one	2 mins
retrieve an object from the pool floor and return it to the poolside	eyes open	one by one	4 mins
Exit: using the pool steps or over the poolside	take your time	one by one	1 min

Total time: 28 minutes

Lesson #73 Assessment

Lesson Objective: to develop and progress basic backstroke arm technique		
Below average	**Average**	**Above average**
😐	🙂	😎
Attempts to demonstrate but does not show the correct technique	**Able to perform most of the technique correctly some of the time**	**Performs the technique correctly most of the time**

Assessment	😐	🙂	😎
Arm pulls are continuous and alternating			
Hand enters the water little finger first			
Fingers are together			
Arms are straight on entry			
Hand enters the water inline with the shoulder			

Lesson Plan #74

Lesson type: backstroke arms
Level: adult or child advanced
Previous learning: full stroke backstroke
Lesson aim: to develop and fine-tune backstroke arm action
Equipment: hand paddles

Exercise/Activity	Teaching Points	Organisation	Duration
Entry: sitting or shallow dive entry	take your time	waves	1 min
Warm up: 2 lengths any stroke	take your time	all together	3 mins
Main Theme: 2 lengths full stroke backstroke	let your movements flow	waves	3 mins
single arm pull with one arm held by the side (opposite arm on return)	thumb exists first	waves	3 mins
alternating arm pulls with a pull buoy held between the legs	one arm pulls and the other recovers	waves	3 mins
single arm pulls using a lane rope to help simulate bent arm pull technique	pull through your body line	waves	3 mins
Repeat any previous drills using hand paddles	pull through to the thigh	waves	3 mins
2 lengths full stroke backstroke	continuous flowing strokes	waves	3 mins
Contrasting Activity: feet first sculling	feet remain at the surface	waves	3 mins
basic racing start	head tucked down on entry	one at a time	3 mins
Exit: using the pool steps or over the poolside	take your time	waves	1 min

Total time: 29 minutes

Lesson #74 Assessment

Lesson Objective: to develop and fine-tune backstroke arm action		
Below average	**Average**	**Above average**
😐	🙂	😎
Attempts to demonstrate but does not show the correct technique	Able to perform most of the technique correctly some of the time	Performs the technique correctly most of the time

Assessment	😐	🙂	😎
Arm pulls are continuous and alternating			
Hand enters the water little finger first			
Fingers are together			
Arms are straight on entry			
Hand enters the water inline with the shoulder			

Lesson Plan #75

Lesson type: backstroke breathing
Level: adult or child beginner
Previous learning: basic back paddle
Lesson aim: to learn basic backstroke breathing technique
Equipment: floats, kickboards and buoyancy aids as necessary

Exercise/Activity	Teaching Points	Organisation	Duration
Entry: pool steps or swivel entry	enter slowly	all together	1 min
Warm up: 2 widths any stroke using buoyancy aids	take your time	all together	2 mins
Main Theme: kicking supine with a woggle under the arms	relax and breathe	all together	2 mins
supine push and glide, holding floats if needed	breathe out as you push off	waves	3 mins
supine kicking with a float held on the chest	continuous breathing	waves	3 mins
single arm pulls with a float held on the chest	breathe out as you pull	waves	3 mins
single arm pulls using the opposite arm with a float held on the chest	breathe out as you pull	waves	3 mins
2 widths full stroke backstroke	steady continuous breathing	waves	3 mins
Contrasting Activity: pencil jump	jump away from the side	all together	2 mins
tuck float (timed)	deep breath, chin to chest	all together	2 mins
Exit: using the pool steps	take your time	one by one	1 min

Total time: 26 minutes

Lesson #75 Assessment

Lesson Objective: to learn basic backstroke breathing technique		
Below average	**Average**	**Above average**
😐	🙂	😎
Attempts to demonstrate but does not show the correct technique	Able to perform most of the technique correctly some of the time	Performs the technique correctly most of the time

Assessment	😐	🙂	😎
Breathing is continuous			
Breathing is relaxed and unlabored*			

*allowances should be made for a swimmer's fitness and stamina levels, as these will affect breathing pattern and continuity.

Lesson Plan #76

Lesson type: backstroke breathing

Level: adult or child intermediate
Previous learning: basic backstroke technique
Lesson aim: to develop breathing technique while performing the full stroke
Equipment: floats, buoyancy aids and hoop

Exercise/Activity	Teaching Points	Organisation	Duration
Entry: swivel entry	enter slowly	all together	1 min
Warm up: 2 widths any stroke	slow and gentle swim	all together	3 mins
Main Theme: 2 widths full stroke backstroke	continuous arms and legs	waves	3 mins
supine push and glide from the poolside	breathe out slowly	waves	3 mins
kicking with float held on the chest	relaxed and steady	waves	3 mins
single arm pull, holding a float on the chest	exhale as you pull	waves	3 mins
repeat above exercise with the opposite arm	inhale as your arm recovers	waves	3 mins
full stroke, breathing in with one pull and out with the other	breathe in and out through your mouth	waves	3 mins
Contrasting Activity: push and glide through a submerged hoop	relax and stretch	2 or 3 at a time	3 mins
treading water for 60 seconds	mouth and nose out of the water	all together	2 mins
Exit: using the pool steps or over the poolside	take your time	one by one/all together	1 min

Total time: 28 minutes

Lesson #76 Assessment

Lesson Objective: to develop breathing technique while performing the full stroke		
Below average	**Average**	**Above average**
😐	🙂	😎
Attempts to demonstrate but does not show the correct technique	**Able to perform most of the technique correctly some of the time**	**Performs the technique correctly most of the time**

Assessment	😐	🙂	😎
Breathing is continuous			
Breathing is relaxed and unlabored*			
Breathing in and out follows arm cycles			

*allowances should be made for a swimmer's fitness and stamina levels, as these will affect breathing pattern and continuity.

Lesson Plan #77

Lesson type: backstroke breathing
Level: adult or child advanced
Previous learning: full stroke backstroke
Lesson aim: to develop and perfect backstroke breathing technique
Equipment: floats and/or kickboard if needed

Exercise/Activity	Teaching Points	Organisation	Duration
Entry: sitting or shallow dive entry	take your time	waves	1 min
Warm up: 2 lengths any stroke	take your time	all together	3 mins
Main Theme: 2 lengths full stroke backstroke	steady breathing	waves	2 mins
supine push and glide with arms extended	exhale as you glide	waves	3 mins
supine kicking with arms extended	breathe out slowly	waves	3 mins
single arm pulls using a lane rope to help simulate bent arm pull technique	pull and blow	waves	3 mins
2 lengths full stroke backstroke with steady rhythmical breathing	exhale as one arm pulls, inhale as the opposite arm pulls	waves	3 mins
2 lengths full stroke backstroke	continuous rhythmical breathing	waves	3 mins
Contrasting Activity: treading water - vary with 1 arm behind the back or above the water	ears and mouth above the surface	waves	3 mins
basic racing start	push hard from the legs	waves	3 mins
Exit: using the pool steps or over the poolside	take your time	one by one	1 min

Total time: 29 minutes

Lesson #77 Assessment

Lesson Objective: to develop and perfect backstroke breathing technique		
Below average	**Average**	**Above average**
😐	🙂	😎
Attempts to demonstrate but does not show the correct technique	**Able to perform most of the technique correctly some of the time**	**Performs the technique correctly most of the time**

Assessment	😐	🙂	😎
Breathing is continuous			
Breathing is relaxed and unlabored*			
Inhalation takes place as one arm pulls			
Exhalation takes place as opposite are pulls			
Breathing is continuous and rhythmical			

*allowances should be made for a swimmer's fitness and stamina levels, as these will affect breathing pattern and continuity.

Lesson Plan #78

Lesson type: backstroke timing and coordination
Level: adult or child beginner
Previous learning: basic back paddle and backstroke arm movement
Lesson aim: to learn basic coordination of arms and legs for backstroke
Equipment: floats, buoyancy aids and sinkers as necessary

Exercise/Activity	Teaching Points	Organisation	Duration
Entry: swivel entry	enter slowly	all together	1 min
Warm up: 2 widths any stroke using buoyancy aids	slow and gentle swim	all together	3 mins
Main Theme: 2 widths back paddle, using arms and legs	continuous kicking	waves	3 mins
supine push and glide adding leg kicks	count 3 kicks at a time	waves	3 mins
single arm pull, holding a float on the chest	3 kicks per arm pull	waves	3 mins
repeat above exercise with the opposite arm	count to 3 with each arm pull	waves	3 mins
push and glide adding arm pulls	continuous arms	waves	3 mins
full stroke, 3 kicks for each arm pull	continuous kicking as you pull	waves	3 mins
Contrasting Activity: prone star float	deep breath and relax	all together	2 mins
submerge to collect an object	eyes open	2 or 3 at a time	3 mins
Exit: using the pool steps or over the poolside	take your time	one by one	1 min

Total time: 28minutes

Lesson #78 Assessment

Lesson Objective: to learn basic coordination of arms and legs for backstroke		
Below average	**Average**	**Above average**
😐	🙂	😎
Attempts to demonstrate but does not show the correct technique	**Able to perform most of the technique correctly some of the time**	**Performs the technique correctly most of the time**

Assessment	😐	🙂	😎
Leg kicks are alternating			
Arm pulls are alternating			
Arms pulls and leg kicks balance each other			

Lesson Plan #79

Lesson type: backstroke timing and coordination
Level: adult or child intermediate
Previous learning: basic timing technique
Lesson aim: to progress and develop previous learning of backstroke timing
Equipment: floats if needed and hoop

Exercise/Activity	Teaching Points	Organisation	Duration
Entry: swivel or sitting dive entry	enter slowly	waves/ all together	1 min
Warm up: 2 widths any stroke	take your time	all together	3 mins
Main Theme: 2 widths full stroke backstroke	count 3 kicks at a time	all together	2 mins
single arm pull, holding a float on the chest	3 kicks per arm pull	waves	3 mins
repeat above exercise with the opposite arm	count to 3 with each arm pull	waves	3 mins
push and glide adding leg kicks	count 3 kicks at a time	waves	3 mins
backstroke catch-up (arms extended, one pull at a time)	maintain a kick and pull rhythm	waves	3 mins
full stroke, 3 kicks for each arm pull	continuous kicking as you pull	waves	3 mins
Contrasting Activity: feet first surface dives through a submerged hoop	stretch up and sink	one by one	4 mins
feet first sculling	toes at the surface	waves	3 mins
Exit: using the pool steps	take your time	one by one	1 min

Total time: 29 minutes

Lesson #79 Assessment

Lesson Objective: to progress and develop previous learning of backstroke timing		
Below average	**Average**	**Above average**
😐	🙂	😎
Attempts to demonstrate but does not show the correct technique	**Able to perform most of the technique correctly some of the time**	**Performs the technique correctly most of the time**

Assessment	😐	🙂	😎
Leg kicks are alternating			
Arm pulls are alternating			
Arms pulls and leg kicks balance each other			
Timing is regular and rhythmical			

Lesson Plan #80

Lesson type: backstroke timing and coordination
Level: adult or child advanced
Previous learning: full stroke backstroke
Lesson aim: to develop and fine-tune backstroke timing
Equipment: floats and sinkers if needed, fins

Exercise/Activity	Teaching Points	Organisation	Duration
Entry: sitting or shallow dive entry	take your time	waves	1 min
Warm up: 2 lengths any stroke	take your time	all together	3 mins
Main Theme: 1 length full stroke backstroke	slow and steady	all together	2 mins
using fins, swim slow motion backstroke	smooth flowing movements	waves	3 mins
using fins, steady pace backstroke	let the legs balance the arms	waves	3 mins
arm pulls with pull buoy between the legs	continuous arms	waves	3 mins
push and glide, add arm pulls and leg kicks	continuous kicking	waves	3 mins
full stroke backstroke, 3 kicks for each arm pull	smooth and balanced	waves	3 mins
Contrasting Activity: head first surface dive and swim underwater for a pre-set distance	deep breath and dig down deep	one by one	3 mins
basic grab start	fast transition to stroke	waves	3 mins
Exit: using the pool steps	take your time	one by one	1 min

Total time: 28 minutes

Lesson #80 Assessment

Lesson Objective: to develop and fine-tune backstroke timing

Below average	Average	Above average
😐	🙂	😎
Attempts to demonstrate but does not show the correct technique	Able to perform most of the technique correctly some of the time	Performs the technique correctly most of the time

Assessment	😐	🙂	😎
Leg kicks are continuous and alternating			
Arm pulls are continuous and alternating			
Arms pulls and leg kicks balance each other			
Timing is regular and rhythmical			

Lesson Plan #81

Lesson type: full stroke butterfly
Level: adult or child beginner
Previous learning: basic front paddle
Lesson aim: to learn the basics of butterfly and experience the whole stroke
Equipment: woggle, buoyancy aids if needed and hoop

Exercise/Activity	Teaching Points	Organisation	Duration
Entry: swivel or steps entry	enter slowly	all together	1 min
Warm up: 2 widths any stroke with buoyancy aids if needed	take your time	all together	3 mins
Main Theme: standing on the poolside showing hip movement	pretend you are a belly dancer	all together	2 mins
push and glide adding leg kicks, use a woggle if needed	legs together	waves	3 mins
push and glide adding arm pulls	arms enter together	waves	3 mins
push and glide with woggle if needed - add arms, legs and breathing	blow out into the water	waves	3 mins
push and glide adding arm pulls and leg kicks	2 kicks to one arm pull	waves	3 mins
2 widths full stroke butterfly	kick and pull continuously	waves	3 mins
Contrasting Activity: prone star float	deep breath and relax	2 or 3 at a time	3 mins
sitting dive through a hoop at the surface	head tucked down	2 or 3 at a time	3 mins
Exit: using the pool steps or over the poolside	take your time	one by one	1 min

Total time: 28 minutes

172

Lesson #81 Assessment

Lesson Objective: to learn each part of basic butterfly and experience the whole stroke

Below average	Average	Above average
😐	🙂	😎
Attempts to demonstrate but does not show the correct technique	Able to perform most of the technique correctly some of the time	Performs the technique correctly most of the time

Assessment	😐	🙂	😎
Face is submerged			
Hips attempt to undulate			
Legs kick together			
Arms enter together			
Attempts 2 kicks to 1 arm pull			

Lesson Plan #82

Lesson type: full stroke butterfly

Level: adult or child intermediate
Previous learning: basic butterfly technique
Lesson aim: to progress and develop the whole stroke to an intermediate level
Equipment: woggle, pull buoy, sinkers and hoop

Exercise/Activity	Teaching Points	Organisation	Duration
Entry: swivel or sitting dive entry	enter slowly	waves	1 min
Warm up: 2 widths any stroke	take your time	all together	2 mins
Main Theme: 2 widths full stroke butterfly with buoyancy aids if needed	pull and kick continuously	waves	3 mins
push and glide adding hip movements	move like a mermaid	one by one	3 mins
leg kicks, using a woggle under the body if needed	slight knee bend	waves	3 mins
arm pulls without kicking, using a woggle if needed	thumb and finger enter first	waves	3 mins
push and glide adding arm pulls and leg kicks	kick your arms in, then kick your arms out	waves	3 mins
full stroke butterfly without buoyancy aids	your head leads the movement	waves	3 mins
Contrasting Activity: head first surface dives, collecting sinkers placed apart	deep breath and dig down	one by one	3 mins
dolphin kick through a hoop at the surface	swim like a mermaid	one by one	3 mins
Exit: using the pool steps or over the poolside	take your time	one by one	1 min

Total time: 28 minutes

Lesson #82 Assessment

Lesson Objective: to progress and develop the whole stroke to an intermediate level		
Below average	**Average**	**Above average**
😐	🙂	😎
Attempts to demonstrate but does not show the correct technique	**Able to perform most of the technique correctly some of the time**	**Performs the technique correctly most of the time**

Assessment	😐	🙂	😎
Undulating movement comes from the head			
Hips undulate continuously			
Legs kick with a slight knee bend			
Hands enter finger and thumb first			
Attempts to 'kick, pull, kick, recover'			

Lesson Plan #83

Lesson type: full stroke butterfly
Level: adult or child advanced
Previous learning: full stroke butterfly
Lesson aim: to develop and fine-tune whole stroke technique
Equipment: floats if needed, sinkers and fins

Exercise/Activity	Teaching Points	Organisation	Duration
Entry: sitting or shallow dive entry	take your time	waves	1 min
Warm up: 2 lengths any stroke	take your time	all together	3 mins
Main Theme: 2 lengths full stroke butterfly	smooth strokes	waves	2 mins
push and glide underwater, adding undulating movement	head leads the movement	waves	3 mins
kicking with arms extended, using fins	move like a dolphin tail	waves	3 mins
arm action using fins on the feet	pull with power	waves	3 mins
full stroke, breathing every stroke	pull your head up	waves	3 mins
2 lengths full stroke butterfly	kick, pull, kick, recover	waves	3 mins
Contrasting Activity: feet-first surface dives to collect an object	stretch up and then sink	waves	3 mins
treading water	head above the water	waves	3 mins
Exit: using the pool steps or over the poolside	take your time	one by one	1 min

Total time: 28 minutes

Lesson #83 Assessment

Lesson Objective: to develop and fine-tune whole stroke technique		
Below average	**Average**	**Above average**
😐	🙂	😎
Attempts to demonstrate but does not show the correct technique	Able to perform most of the technique correctly some of the time	Performs the technique correctly most of the time

Assessment	😐	🙂	😎
Undulating movement comes from the head			
Legs kick continuously and with power			
Hands enter finger and thumb first			
Arms recover low over the water surface			
inhalation takes place as the arms outsweep			
Timing pattern follows 'kick, pull, kick, recover'			

Lesson Plan #84

Lesson type: butterfly body position
Level: adult or child beginner
Previous learning: basic front paddle and push and glide
Lesson aim: to learn basic body position and movement
Equipment: buoyancy aids if needed

Exercise/Activity	Teaching Points	Organisation	Duration
Entry: swivel entry	enter slowly	all together	1 min
Warm up: 2 widths any stroke using buoyancy aids	slow and gentle swim	all together	3 mins
Main Theme: standing on the poolside showing hip movement	pretend you are a belly dancer	all together	2 mins
holding the poolside, slow dolphin kick action	make your body into a long wave	all together	2 mins
dolphin dives whilst walking though the water	stretch up to the surface	waves	4 mins
push and glide with arms by the sides, adding undulating movement	lead with your head	waves	3 mins
push and glide adding dolphin kicks	pretend you are a dolphin	waves	3 mins
2 widths dolphin kick, arms by the sides	face down	waves	3 mins
Contrasting Activity: supine push and glide	feet together and toes pointed	waves	2 mins
sitting dive	head tucked down	one by one	3 mins
Exit: using the pool steps or over the poolside	take your time	one by one	1 min

Total time: 27minutes

Lesson #84 Assessment

Lesson Objective: to learn basic butterfly body position and movement

Below average	Average	Above average
😐	🙂	😎
Attempts to demonstrate but does not show the correct technique	Able to perform most of the technique correctly some of the time	Performs the technique correctly most of the time

Assessment	😐	🙂	😎
Body moves in a wave-like action			
Head leads the movement			
Legs and feet are together			
Hips are level			
Shoulders are level			

Lesson Plan #85

Lesson type: butterfly body position

Level: adult or child intermediate
Previous learning: basic butterfly butterfly technique
Lesson aim: to improve basic butterfly body position and movement
Equipment: buoyancy aids if needed and hoop

Exercise/Activity	Teaching Points	Organisation	Duration
Entry: swivel entry	enter slowly	all together	1 min
Warm up: 2 widths any stroke without using buoyancy aids	take your time	all together	3 mins
Main Theme: 2 widths full stroke butterfly	continuous arms and legs	waves	3 mins
dolphin dives whilst walking though the water	stretch up to the surface	waves	3 mins
push and glide with arms by the sides, adding undulating movement	lead with your head	waves	3 mins
supine push and glide with arms by the sides, adding undulating movement	make your hips undulate	waves	3 mins
push and glide with arms extended, adding dolphin kicks	pretend you are a dolphin	waves	3 mins
2 widths full stroke butterfly	continuous arms and legs	waves	3 mins
Contrasting Activity: forward somersault from a push and glide	tuck chin on chest	2 or 3 at a time	3 mins
sitting dive through a submerged hoop	hands together	2 or 3 at a time	3 mins
Exit: using the pool steps or over the poolside	take your time	one by one	1 min

Total time: 29 minutes

Lesson #85 Assessment

Lesson Objective: to improve basic butterfly body position and movement		
Below average	**Average**	**Above average**
😐	🙂	😎
Attempts to demonstrate but does not show the correct technique	Able to perform most of the technique correctly some of the time	Performs the technique correctly most of the time

Assessment	😐	🙂	😎
Head leads the movement			
Body movement is undulating			
Legs and feet are together			
Hands are together when extended			
Hips and shoulders are level			

Lesson Plan #86

Lesson type: butterfly body position
Level: adult or child advanced
Previous learning: full stroke butterfly
Lesson aim: to develop and fine-tune butterfly body position and movement
Equipment: buoyancy aids if needed

Exercise/Activity	Teaching Points	Organisation	Duration
Entry: sitting or shallow dive entry	take your time	all together	1 min
Warm up: 2 lengths any stroke	steady pace	all together	3 mins
Main Theme: 2 lengths full stroke butterfly	let the stroke flow	all together	3 mins
push and glide with arms extended, adding undulating movement	make your hips undulate	waves	3 mins
supine push and glide with arms extended, adding undulating movement	wave-like body movement	waves	3 mins
push and glide underwater with arms extended, adding dolphin kicks	pretend you are a dolphin	waves	3 mins
push and glide adding leg kicks, measure distance covered	maintain a streamlined shape	waves	3 mins
2 lengths full stroke butterfly from racing start	let your head drive the body action	waves	3 mins
Contrasting Activity: prone push and glide and rotate to supine position	keep head level	2 or 3 at a time	3 mins
any stroke with somersault mid swim	head down, chin to chest	2 or 3 at a time	3 mins
Exit: using the pool steps or over the poolside	take your time	all together	1 min

Total time: 29 minutes

Lesson #86 Assessment

Lesson Objective: to develop and fine-tune butterfly body position and movement		
Below average	**Average**	**Above average**
😐	🙂	😎
Attempts to demonstrate but does not show the correct technique	**Able to perform most of the technique correctly some of the time**	**Performs the technique correctly most of the time**

Assessment	😐	🙂	😎
Head leads the movement			
Body movement is continuous and undulating			
Legs and feet are together			
Hands are together when extended			
Hips and shoulders are level			
Body movement is smooth and flowing			

Lesson Plan #87

Lesson type: butterfly leg kick
Level: adult or child beginner
Previous learning: basic front paddle and submerging
Lesson aim: to learn basic dolphin kick action
Equipment: floats and buoyancy aids if needed

Exercise/Activity	Teaching Points	Organisation	Duration
Entry: swivel entry	enter slowly	all together	1 min
Warm up: 2 widths any stroke using buoyancy aids	slow and gentle swim	all together	3 mins
Main Theme: sitting on the poolside, legs in the water	kick out like you are on a swing	all together	2 mins
holding the poolside, slow dolphin kick action	kick like a mermaid	all together	2 mins
dolphin leg kicks - holding a float if needed	show your dolphin tail	waves	3 mins
push and glide adding dolphin kicks	kick with both legs together	waves	3 mins
dolphin kick in a supine position	flick your feet upwards	waves	3 mins
2 widths dolphin kick, arms by the sides	face down	waves	3 mins
Contrasting Activity: supine star float	relax and stretch	all together	3 mins
pencil jump	jump outwards	one by one	3 mins
Exit: using the pool steps or over the poolside	take your time	one by one	1 min

Total time: 27 minutes

Lesson #87 Assessment

Lesson Objective: to learn basic dolphin kick action		
Below average	**Average**	**Above average**
😐	🙂	😎
Attempts to demonstrate but does not show the correct technique	**Able to perform most of the technique correctly some of the time**	**Performs the technique correctly most of the time**

Assessment	😐	🙂	😎
Legs kicks are simultaneous			
Toes are pointed			
Legs remain together			
Kick comes from body movement			

Lesson Plan #88

Lesson type: butterfly leg kick
Level: adult or child intermediate
Previous learning: basic butterfly technique
Lesson aim: to strengthen and develop basic butterfly leg kick
Equipment: buoyancy aids if needed and hoop

Exercise/Activity	Teaching Points	Organisation	Duration
Entry: swivel or sitting dive entry	enter slowly	all together	1 min
Warm up: 2 widths any stroke	take your time	all together	3 mins
Main Theme: 2 widths full stroke butterfly	let the stroke flow	waves	2 mins
push and glide adding dolphin kicks	kick with both legs together	waves	3 mins
dolphin kick in a supine position	flick your feet upwards	waves	3 mins
kick and roll, arms by the sides	head leads the movement	waves	3 mins
2 widths dolphin kick, arms extended	kick with power	waves	3 mins
2 widths full stroke butterfly	relaxed, flowing kicks	waves	3 mins
Contrasting Activity: sitting dives	chin to chest	one by one	3 mins
push and glide through a submerged hoop	hands and feet together	one by one	3 mins
Exit: using the pool steps	take your time	one by one	1 min

Total time: 28 minutes

Lesson #88 Assessment

Lesson Objective: to strengthen and develop basic butterfly leg kick		
Below average	**Average**	**Above average**
😐	🙂	😎
Attempts to demonstrate but does not show the correct technique	Able to perform most of the technique correctly some of the time	Performs the technique correctly most of the time

Assessment	😐	🙂	😎
Legs kicks are simultaneous with legs together			
Toes are pointed with ankles relaxed			
Legs kick with power			
Kick comes from body movement			

Lesson Plan #89

Lesson type: butterfly leg kick
Level: adult or child advanced
Previous learning: full stroke butterfly
Lesson aim: to develop and perfect butterfly leg kick
Equipment: kickboards if needed and fins

Exercise/Activity	Teaching Points	Organisation	Duration
Entry: sitting or shallow dive entry	take your time	waves	1 min
Warm up: 2 lengths any stroke	take your time	all together	3 mins
Main Theme: 2 lengths full stroke butterfly	smooth flowing movements	waves	3 mins
push and glide adding dolphin kicks with arms extended	kick like a dolphin tail	waves	3 mins
dolphin kick with fins	kick with power	waves	3 mins
dolphin kick on the side with arms extended - add optional fins	flick your feet	waves	3 mins
supine dolphin kick with arms extended - add optional fins	slight bend of the knees	waves	3 mins
2 widths full stroke butterfly	relaxed, flowing kicks	waves	3 mins
Contrasting Activity: push and glide into forward somersault	arms pull down to rotate	2 or 3 at a time	2 mins
supine push and glide into somersault	tuck chin to chest	2 or 3 at a time	2 mins
Exit: using the pool steps	take your time	waves	1 min

Total time: 27 minutes

Lesson #89 Assessment

Lesson Objective: to develop and perfect butterfly leg kick		
Below average	**Average**	**Above average**
😐	🙂	😎
Attempts to demonstrate but does not show the correct technique	**Able to perform most of the technique correctly some of the time**	**Performs the technique correctly most of the time**

Assessment	😐	🙂	😎
Toes are pointed with ankles relaxed			
Knee bend is minimal			
Legs kick with power			
Kick comes from body movement			
Kicks are smooth and flowing			

Lesson Plan #90

Lesson type: butterfly arms
Level: adult or child beginner
Previous learning: basic front paddle
Lesson aim: to learn basic butterfly arm action
Equipment: buoyancy aids if needed and hoop

Exercise/Activity	Teaching Points	Organisation	Duration
Entry: swivel entry	enter slowly	all together	1 min
Warm up: 2 widths any stroke using buoyancy aids	slow and gentle swim	all together	3 mins
Main Theme: standing on the poolside, basic arm movement	both arms at the same time	all together	2 mins
walking through water, basic arm movement	pull back together	all together	3 mins
push and glide adding arm movements	make a keyhole shape	waves	3 mins
push and glide adding arm and leg movements	thumb enters first	waves	3 mins
supine dolphin kick adding double arms	kick and pull	waves	3 mins
2 widths full stroke	pull and kick with power	waves	3 mins
Contrasting Activity: sitting dive though a surface hoop	chin tucked down	one by one	3 mins
sitting dive though a submerged hoop	push off and stretch	one by one	3 mins
Exit: using the pool steps or over the poolside	take your time	one by one	1 min

Total time: 28 minutes

Lesson #90 Assessment

Lesson Objective: to learn and practice basic butterfly arm pull		
Below average	**Average**	**Above average**
😐	🙂	😎
Attempts to demonstrate but does not show the correct technique	Able to perform most of the technique correctly some of the time	Performs the technique correctly most of the time

Assessment	😐	🙂	😎
Arm pulls are simultaneous			
Hand enters the water thumb and finger first			
Fingers are together			
Arms recover simultaneously			

Lesson Plan #91

Lesson type: butterfly arms
Level: adult or child intermediate
Previous learning: basic butterfly technique
Lesson aim: to develop and progress butterfly arm technique
Equipment: buoyancy aids if need, fins and sinkers

Exercise/Activity	Teaching Points	Organisation	Duration
Entry: swivel entry or sitting dive entry	take your time	all together	1 min
Warm up: 2 widths any stroke	continuous swimming	all together	2 mins
Main Theme: 2 widths full stroke butterfly	relaxed, smooth movements	waves	3 mins
push and glide adding arm movements	thumb enters first	waves	3 mins
push and glide adding arm pulls with an underwater recovery	make a keyhole shape	waves	3 mins
push and glide adding arm pulls, kicking with fins to add support	hands accelerate through the water	waves	3 mins
2 widths kicking adding arm pulls (with optional fins)	arms recover low over the water	waves	3 mins
2 widths full stroke butterfly	arms and legs move together	waves	3 mins
Contrasting Activity: treading water	mouth and nose out of the water	one by one	2 mins
retrieve an object from the pool floor and return it to the poolside	eyes open	one by one	4 mins
Exit: using the pool steps or over the poolside	take your time	one by one	1 min

Total time: 28 minutes

Lesson #91 Assessment

Lesson Objective: to develop and progress basic butterfly arm action		
Below average	**Average**	**Above average**
😐	🙂	😎
Attempts to demonstrate but does not show the correct technique	Able to perform most of the technique correctly some of the time	Performs the technique correctly most of the time

Assessment	😐	🙂	😎
Arm pulls are simultaneous			
Hand enter in line with the shoulders			
Hands pull in a keyhole shape			
Arms recover low over the water surface			
Fingers remain together throughout			

Lesson Plan #92

Lesson type: butterfly arms
Level: adult or child advanced
Previous learning: full stroke butterfly
Lesson aim: to develop and fine-tune butterfly arm action
Equipment: hand paddles and fins if needed

Exercise/Activity	Teaching Points	Organisation	Duration
Entry: sitting or shallow dive entry	take your time	waves	1 min
Warm up: 2 lengths any stroke	take your time	all together	3 mins
Main Theme: 2 lengths full stroke butterfly	let your movements flow	waves	3 mins
push and glide adding arm movements, counting arm pull over a short distance	hands enter inline with shoulders	waves	3 mins
push and glide adding arm pulls, using hand paddles	hands accelerate through the water	waves	3 mins
2 widths kicking adding arm pulls, counting arm pulls (with optional fins)	arms recover low over the water	waves	3 mins
Repeat previous drill maintaining or reducing number of arm pulls	fast and relaxed arm action	waves	3 mins
2 widths full stroke butterfly	smooth flowing movements	waves	3 mins
Contrasting Activity: feet first sculling	feet remain at the surface	waves	3 mins
basic racing start	head tucked down on entry	one at a time	3 mins
Exit: using the pool steps or over the poolside	take your time	waves	1 min

Total time: 29 minutes

Lesson #92 Assessment

Below average	Average	Above average
🙂	🙂	😎
Attempts to demonstrate but does not show the correct technique	Able to perform most of the technique correctly some of the time	Performs the technique correctly most of the time

Lesson Objective: to develop and fine-tune butterfly arm action

Assessment	🙂	🙂	😎
Arm pulls are relaxed and continuous			
Hands accelerate though the water			
Hands pull in a keyhole shape			
Arms recover low over the water surface			
Hands enter in line with the shoulders			

Lesson Plan #93

Lesson type: butterfly breathing

Level: adult or child beginner
Previous learning: front paddle, including breathing and submerging
Lesson aim: to learn basic butterfly breathing technique
Equipment: buoyancy aids if needed

Exercise/Activity	Teaching Points	Organisation	Duration
Entry: swivel entry	enter slowly	all together	1 min
Warm up: 2 widths any stroke using buoyancy aids	slow and gentle swim	all together	3 mins
Main Theme: standing on the poolside showing arm action with breathing	chin up as your pull back	all together	2 mins
walking through water, arm action with breathing	blow out into the water	all together	3 mins
dolphin kicks breathing every 4 kicks	breathe out slowly	waves	3 mins
push and glide adding kicks and breathing	1-2-3 breathe	waves	3 mins
full stroke breathing every stroke	inhale as your arms recover	waves	3 mins
full stroke breathing every other stroke	blow out hard as you lift your head	waves	3 mins
Contrasting Activity: tuck (mushroom) float	knees and chin to chest	all together	2 mins
pencil jump	jump away from the poolside	one by one	3 mins
Exit: using the pool steps or over the poolside	take your time	one by one	1 min

Total time: 27 minutes

Lesson #93 Assessment

Lesson Objective: to learn basic butterfly breathing technique		
Below average	**Average**	**Above average**
😐	🙂	😎
Attempts to demonstrate but does not show the correct technique	Able to perform most of the technique correctly some of the time	Performs the technique correctly most of the time

Assessment	😐	🙂	😎
Breathing is in time with the arm cycle			
Exhalation takes place in the water			
Inhalation takes place as the arms recover			

Lesson Plan #94

Lesson type: butterfly breathing
Level: adult or child intermediate
Previous learning: basic butterfly technique
Lesson aim: to develop breathing technique while performing the full stroke
Equipment: buoyancy aids if needed and hoop

Exercise/Activity	Teaching Points	Organisation	Duration
Entry: swivel entry	enter slowly	all together	1 min
Warm up: 2 widths any stroke	slow and gentle swim	all together	3 mins
Main Theme: 2 widths full stroke butterfly	continuous arms and legs	waves	3 mins
push and glide adding arm pulls, breathing every other pull	control your breath	waves	3 mins
dolphin kicks breathing every 2 kicks	kick, kick, breathe	waves	3 mins
dolphin kick with breaststroke arms, breathing every stroke	kick and blow	waves	3 mins
full stroke breathing every other stroke	blow out hard as you lift your head	waves	3 mins
full stroke breathing every stroke	inhale at the end of your arm pull	waves	3 mins
Contrasting Activity: push and glide through a submerged hoop	relax and stretch	2 or 3 at a time	3 mins
treading water for 60 seconds	mouth and nose out of the water	all together	2 mins
Exit: using the pool steps or over the poolside	take your time	one by one/all together	1 min

Total time: 28 minutes

Lesson #94 Assessment

Lesson Objective: to develop breathing technique while performing the full stroke		
Below average	**Average**	**Above average**
😐	🙂	😎
Attempts to demonstrate but does not show the correct technique	**Able to perform most of the technique correctly some of the time**	**Performs the technique correctly most of the time**

Assessment	😐	🙂	😎
Breathing is in time with the arm cycle			
Exhalation takes place in the water			
Inhalation takes place as the arms recover			
Breathing is continuous and unlabored*			

*allowances should be made for a swimmer's fitness and stamina levels, as these will affect breathing pattern and continuity.

Lesson Plan #95

Lesson type: butterfly breathing
Level: adult or child advanced
Previous learning: full stroke butterfly
Lesson aim: to develop and perfect butterfly breathing technique
Equipment: kickboard if needed and fins

Exercise/Activity	Teaching Points	Organisation	Duration
Entry: sitting or shallow dive entry	take your time	waves	1 min
Warm up: 2 lengths any stroke	take your time	all together	3 mins
Main Theme: 2 lengths full stroke butterfly	steady breathing	waves	2 mins
dolphin kicks using fins, breathing every 2 kicks	kick, kick, breathe	waves	3 mins
dolphin kick with breaststroke arms, breathing every other stroke	slow controlled breathing	waves	3 mins
full stroke with fins, breathing every other stroke	blow out hard as you lift your head	waves	3 mins
2 lengths full stroke - breathing every stroke	inhale at the end of your arm pull	waves	3 mins
2 lengths full stroke butterfly	continuous rhythmical breathing	waves	3 mins
Contrasting Activity: treading water - vary with 1 arm behind the back or above the water	ears and mouth above the surface	waves	3 mins
basic racing start	push hard from the legs	waves	3 mins
Exit: using the pool steps or over the poolside	take your time	one by one	1 min

Total time: 29 minutes

Lesson #95 Assessment

Lesson Objective: to develop and perfect butterfly breathing technique		
Below average	**Average**	**Above average**
😐	🙂	😎
Attempts to demonstrate but does not show the correct technique	**Able to perform most of the technique correctly some of the time**	**Performs the technique correctly most of the time**

Assessment	😐	🙂	😎
Breathing is in time with the arm cycle			
Exhalation takes place in the water			
Inhalation takes place as the arms recover			
Breathing is 'explosive' when performed every stroke			

Lesson Plan #96

Lesson type: butterfly timing and coordination
Level: adult or child beginner
Previous learning: basic back paddle and butterfly arm movement
Lesson aim: to learn basic coordination of arms and legs for butterfly
Equipment: buoyancy aids and sinkers as necessary

Exercise/Activity	Teaching Points	Organisation	Duration
Entry: swivel entry	enter slowly	all together	1 min
Warm up: 2 widths any stroke using buoyancy aids	slow and gentle swim	all together	3 mins
Main Theme: 2 widths full stroke butterfly	arms and legs work together	waves	3 mins
push and glide adding leg kicks	count 2 kicks at a time	waves	3 mins
push and glide adding arm pulls	continuous arms	waves	3 mins
push and glide adding leg kicks and arm pulls - perform slowly at first	2 beat leg kick	waves	3 mins
1 width full stroke butterfly	kick head down, kick head up	waves	3 mins
2 widths full stroke butterfly	kick, pull, kick, recover	waves	3 mins
Contrasting Activity: prone star float	deep breath and relax	all together	2 mins
submerge to collect an object	eyes open	2 or 3 at a time	3 mins
Exit: using the pool steps or over the poolside	take your time	one by one	1 min

Total time: 28minutes

202

Lesson #96 Assessment

Lesson Objective: to learn basic coordination of arms and legs for butterfly		
Below average	**Average**	**Above average**
😐	🙂	😎
Attempts to demonstrate but does not show the correct technique	**Able to perform most of the technique correctly some of the time**	**Performs the technique correctly most of the time**

Assessment	😐	🙂	😎
Arms and legs are continuous			
2 beat leg kick			
Leg kicks are in time with the arm pull cycle			

Lesson Plan #97

Lesson type: butterfly timing and coordination

Level: adult or child intermediate
Previous learning: basic timing technique
Lesson aim: to progress and develop previous learning of butterfly timing
Equipment: buoyancy aids if needed and hoop

Exercise/Activity	Teaching Points	Organisation	Duration
Entry: swivel or sitting dive entry	enter slowly	waves/ all together	1 min
Warm up: 2 widths any stroke	take your time	all together	3 mins
Main Theme: 2 widths full stroke butterfly	arms and legs are continuous	all together	2 mins
push and glide adding leg kicks and arm pulls - perform slowly at first	2 beat leg kick	waves	3 mins
push and glide adding a single stroke cycle	kick the arms in and kick the arms out	waves	3 mins
leg kicks with breaststroke arms	kick, pull, kick, dive	waves	3 mins
1 width full stroke butterfly - perform slowly at first	kick, kick, throw the arms over	waves	3 mins
2 widths full stroke butterfly	kick, pull, kick, recover	waves	3 mins
Contrasting Activity: feet first surface dives through a submerged hoop	stretch up and sink	one by one	4 mins
feet first sculling	toes at the surface	waves	3 mins
Exit: using the pool steps	take your time	one by one	1 min

Total time: 29 minutes

Lesson #97 Assessment

Lesson Objective: to progress and develop previous learning of butterfly timing		
Below average	**Average**	**Above average**
😐	🙂	😎
Attempts to demonstrate but does not show the correct technique	**Able to perform most of the technique correctly some of the time**	**Performs the technique correctly most of the time**

Assessment	😐	🙂	😎
Arms and legs are continuous			
2 beat leg kick			
'Kick, pull, kick, recover' sequence			
Timing is regular and rhythmical			

Lesson Plan #98

Lesson type: butterfly timing and coordination
Level: adult or child advanced
Previous learning: full stroke butterfly
Lesson aim: to develop and fine-tune butterfly timing
Equipment: floats and sinkers if needed, fins

Exercise/Activity	Teaching Points	Organisation	Duration
Entry: sitting or shallow dive entry	take your time	waves	1 min
Warm up: 2 lengths any stroke	take your time	all together	3 mins
Main Theme: 1 length full stroke butterfly	arms and legs are continuous	all together	2 mins
push and glide adding stroke cycles	2 beat leg kick	waves	3 mins
leg kicks with breaststroke arms	kick, pull, kick, dive	waves	3 mins
1 length full stroke butterfly - optional with fins	kick the arms in and kick the arms out	waves	3 mins
1 length full stroke butterfly counting stroke cycles	kick, kick, throw the arms over	waves	3 mins
2 lengths full stroke butterfly	kick, pull, kick, recover	waves	3 mins
Contrasting Activity: head first surface dive and swim underwater for a pre-set distance	deep breath and dig down deep	one by one	3 mins
basic racing start	fast transition to stroke	waves	3 mins
Exit: using the pool steps	take your time	one by one	1 min

Total time: 28 minutes

Lesson #98 Assessment

Lesson Objective: to develop and fine-tune butterfly timing		
Below average	**Average**	**Above average**
😐	🙂	😎
Attempts to demonstrate but does not show the correct technique	Able to perform most of the technique correctly some of the time	Performs the technique correctly most of the time

Assessment	😐	🙂	😎
Arms and legs are continuous			
Kick occurs when the arms pull and then again as the arms recover			
'Kick, pull, kick, recover' sequence			
Timing is regular and rhythmical			

Lesson Plan #99

Lesson type: sidestroke
Level: adult or child intermediate
Previous learning: swimming on the front, either front crawl or breaststroke
Lesson aim: to learn the basics of sidestroke
Equipment: floats

Exercise/Activity	Teaching Points	Organisation	Duration
Entry: sitting or shallow dive entry	take your time	waves	1 min
Warm up: 2 lengths any stroke	take your time	all together	3 mins
Main Theme: push and glide on the side, lower arm extended and upper arm at the side	lay on your side	waves	3 mins
kicking with a float under each arm, one arm extended, the other bent to the side	bend the knee like riding a bicycle	waves	3 mins
arm pulls using the upper arm, float in the extended arm	pull the water to your thigh	waves	3 mins
arm pulls using the extended arm, float in the upper arm	pull the water towards the head	waves	3 mins
push and glide adding one arm pull and one leg kick	upper arm pulls as legs kick together	waves	3 mins
2 lengths full stroke sidestroke	long streamlined glide	waves	3 mins
Contrasting Activity: dolphin kick underwater	relaxed flowing movements	waves	3 mins
head first sculling followed by feet first sculling	head back, toes at the surface	waves	3 mins
Exit: using the pool steps	take your time	one by one	1 min

Total time: 28 minutes

Lesson #99 Assessment

Lesson Objective: to learn the basics of sidestroke		
Below average	**Average**	**Above average**
😐	🙂	😎
Attempts to demonstrate but does not show the correct technique	Able to perform most of the technique correctly some of the time	Performs the technique correctly most of the time

Assessment	😐	🙂	😎
Glide in a side position			
Kick in a scissor-like action			
Kick under and parallel to the water surface			
One arm pulls as the other recovers			
Glide after each stroke cycle			

Lesson Plan #100

Lesson type: survival skills
Level: adult or child intermediate
Previous learning: swimming on the front and back and treading water
Lesson aim: to learn basic survival skills
Equipment: appropriate sinkers

Exercise/Activity	Teaching Points	Organisation	Duration
Entry: swivel entry (as if into unknown waters)	take your time	waves	1 min
Warm up: 2 lengths breaststroke	take your time	all together	3 mins
Main Theme: 1 length life saving backstroke (supine breaststroke legs with arms pushing towards the feet)	simultaneous arm and leg movements	waves	3 mins
1 length sidestroke	glide after each stroke	waves	3 mins
swim a preset distance and perform a head first surface dive	chin to chest and pull strongly	waves	3 mins
swim a preset distance and perform a feet first surface dive	streamlined shape as you sink down	waves	3 mins
swim a preset distance and surface dive to retrieve an object	arms extended when submerging	waves	3 mins
repeat as above - return the object to the starting point using lifesaving backstroke	use one arm on the way back	waves	3 mins
Contrasting Activity: straddle jump	slap down with your hands	waves	3 mins
compact jump	spread arms and legs as you enter	waves	3 mins
Exit: over the poolside (as if from unknown waters)	be mindful of unknown surfaces	one by one	1 min

Total time: 28 minutes

Lesson #100 Assessment

Lesson Objective: to learn basic survival skills		
Below average	**Average**	**Above average**
😐	🙂	😎
Attempts to demonstrate but does not show the correct technique	Able to perform most of the technique correctly some of the time	Performs the technique correctly most of the time

Assessment	😐	🙂	😎
Perform basic sidestroke			
Perform basic lifesaving backstroke			
Perform a head first surface dive			
Perform a feet first surface dive			
Perform a surface dive as part of a longer swim			

Lesson Plan #101

Lesson type: survival skills
Level: adult or child intermediate
Previous learning: swimming confidently on the front and back and treading water
Lesson aim: to develop basic survival skills by swimming in clothing*
Equipment: woggles and appropriate sinkers

Exercise/Activity	Teaching Points	Organisation	Duration
Entry: straddle entry (as if into unknown waters)	step into the water	waves	1 min
Warm up: breaststroke in clothing (shallow water)	keep your head up	all together	2 mins
Main Theme: 1 length life saving backstroke in clothing	kick with power	waves	3 mins
1 length sidestroke in clothing	kick and pull with power	waves	3 mins
swim a preset distance and perform a head first surface dive in clothing	vertical body as your submerge	waves	3 mins
swim a preset distance and perform a feet first surface dive in clothing	streamlined shape as you sink down	waves	3 mins
remove additional clothing in shallow water**	undo buttons and fastenings first	all together	3 mins
swim to a submerged object and return it within a preset time	swim with some urgency	waves	3 mins
Contrasting Activity: use a woggle to perform a reach rescue in shallow water (with a partner)	clear verbal communication	waves	4 mins
rescue a casualty using a contact chin tow (progress to deep water when confident)	approach casualty from behind	waves	4 mins
Exit: over the poolside (as if from unknown waters)	be mindful of unknown surfaces	one by one	1 min

Total time: 30 minutes

*swimmers clothing should be light at first (t-shirt, shorts etc) and then built up accordingly
** removal of clothing should be progressed and preformed in deep water when appropriate

Lesson #101 Assessment

Lesson Objective: to develop basic survival skills by swimming in clothing		
Below average	**Average**	**Above average**
😐	🙂	😎
Attempts to demonstrate but does not show the correct technique	**Able to perform most of the technique correctly some of the time**	**Performs the technique correctly most of the time**

Assessment	😐	🙂	😎
Perform basic sidestroke in clothing			
Perform basic lifesaving backstroke in clothing			
Perform a head first surface dive in clothing			
Perform a feet first surface dive in clothing			
Remove extra clothing whilst in the water			

Lesson Plan

Lesson type:
Level:
Previous learning:
Lesson aim:
Equipment:

	Exercise/Activity	Teaching Points	Organisation	Duration
Entry:				
Warm up:				
Main Theme:				
Contrasting Activity:				
Exit:				

Total time: minutes

Download and print a copy of this blank plan here:

https://www.swim-teach.com/blank-swimming-lesson-plan.html

Lesson #   Assessment

Lesson Objective:		
Below average	**Average**	**Above average**
😐	🙂	😎
Attempts to demonstrate but does not show the correct technique	Able to perform most of the technique correctly some of the time	Performs the technique correctly most of the time

Assessment	😐	🙂	😎

Index of Lesson Plans

Child Beginners

Adult Beginners

Front Crawl

Lesson #27   full stroke - beginners
Lesson #28   full stroke - intermediate
Lesson #29   full stroke - advanced
Lesson #30   body position - beginners
Lesson #31   body position - intermediate
Lesson #32   body position - advanced
Lesson #33   leg kick - beginners
Lesson #34   leg kick - intermediate
Lesson #35   leg kick - advanced
Lesson #36   arm action - beginners
Lesson #37   arm action - intermediate
Lesson #38   arm action - advanced
Lesson #39   breathing - beginners
Lesson #40   breathing - intermediate
Lesson #41   breathing - advanced
Lesson #42   timing - beginners
Lesson #43   timing - intermediate
Lesson #44   timing - advanced

Breaststroke

Lesson #45   full stroke - beginners
Lesson #46   full stroke - intermediate
Lesson #47   full stroke - advanced
Lesson #48   body position - beginners
Lesson #49   body position - intermediate
Lesson #50   body position - advanced
Lesson #51   leg kick - beginners
Lesson #52   leg kick - intermediate
Lesson #53   leg kick - advanced
Lesson #54   arm action - beginners
Lesson #55   arm action - intermediate
Lesson #56   arm action - advanced

Breaststroke continued

Lesson #57	breathing - beginners
Lesson #58	breathing - intermediate
Lesson #59	breathing - advanced
Lesson #60	timing - beginners
Lesson #61	timing - intermediate
Lesson #62	timing - advanced

Backstroke

Lesson #63	full stroke - beginners
Lesson #64	full stroke - intermediate
Lesson #65	full stroke - advanced
Lesson #66	body position - beginners
Lesson #67	body position - intermediate
Lesson #68	body position - advanced
Lesson #69	leg kick - beginners
Lesson #70	leg kick - intermediate
Lesson #71	leg kick - advanced
Lesson #72	arm action - beginners
Lesson #73	arm action - intermediate
Lesson #74	arm action - advanced
Lesson #75	breathing - beginners
Lesson #76	breathing - intermediate
Lesson #77	breathing - advanced
Lesson #78	timing - beginners
Lesson #79	timing - intermediate
Lesson #80	timing - advanced

Butterfly

Lesson #81	full stroke - beginners
Lesson #82	full stroke - intermediate
Lesson #83	full stroke - advanced
Lesson #84	body position - beginners

Butterfly continued

Lesson #85   body position - intermediate
Lesson #86   body position - advanced
Lesson #87   leg kick - beginners
Lesson #88   leg kick - intermediate
Lesson #89   leg kick - advanced
Lesson #90   arm action - beginners
Lesson #91   arm action - intermediate
Lesson #92   arm action - advanced
Lesson #93   breathing - beginners
Lesson #94   breathing - intermediate
Lesson #95   breathing - advanced
Lesson #96   timing - beginners
Lesson #97   timing - intermediate
Lesson #98   timing - advanced

Personal Survival

Lesson #99   sidestroke
Lesson #100   survival skills 1
Lesson #101   survival skills 2

"Now that you have finished my book, would you please consider writing a review? Reviews are the best way readers discover great new books. I would truly appreciate it."

Mark Young

For more information about teaching swimming, learning to swim and improving swimming technique visit **Swim Teach**.

www.swim-teach.com

Made in United States
Orlando, FL
20 June 2024

48089969R00122